Madness. Mania. Miracles.

A story of hope, inspiration and possibility for full recovery
from bipolar disorder, depression and anxiety

ISBN 978-0-578-00054-1

Printed in the United States of America

Book Design by: Andy Choquette
Book Editing by: Sandra Scott

Acknowledgements

Thank you to everyone who played a part in the story of my life as told in the pages of this book. Because of you this book is possible. May love and peace fill all your days.

Thank you to my wonderful, precious supporters who have cheered me on to the finish line. A special acknowledgement to Alexandra Platt for her role as a catalyst to get the book off the shelf and into print and for listening to my musing throughout the process and to Katie Elzer-Peters for the early version editing work she contributed.

Thank you to Doug, my husband, who has stood by me on every step of the journey to wellness. I love you and I'm so grateful to have you in my life.

Thank you to my mom for agreeing to work along side me as we reopened these painful chapters of our life. Her contribution in the pages that follow offers readers the amazing gift of a mother's tender loving hand as she guides us through the journey from her point of view.

Finally, thank you to Me. All aspects of Me: the dark and the light. I am grateful to be home and functioning as unit of one!

Preface

The book you are about to read is written from two points of view—my own and my mother's. To help make the distinction the chapters written by my mother are in italics.

Part One of the book takes you on my journey through madness and during Part Two you join me on my road to wellness. The names of the characters have been changed. No matter what your reaction to the drama and characters of this story please know that I wish only love and peace to everyone who surrounded the events. Forgiving everyone, including myself, has been instrumental in my journey to wholeness.

From time to time you will come across a poem or quote from Sylvia Plath. Sylvia Plath lived from 1932 to 1963. She was a poet, novelist and short story writer who suffered mental breakdown and subsequently committed suicide at age thirty. Much of her writing is confessional in nature and parallels the challenges that we all suffer from inside mental illness.

To eliminate confusion due to my numerous moves, the accompanying drama and destruction that follows I have included a timeline with each chapter to help the reader with a sense of chronology.

The chapters, while many, are short so fasten your seat belt and let the rollercoaster ride begin!

Table of Contents

Introduction

Part One: A Journey through Madness

Part Two: My Journey to Wellness

Afterward: Reflecting on Mental Illness

"The Mind is its own place,
and in itself can make a heaven of hell
and a hell of a heaven."

–John Milton

My Journey

Meet Yourself in the Middle is my personal account of living with bipolar disorder. The book recounts a five-year period of my life. While reading my story, you will travel through three countries, seven cities and into the depths of the wayfarer's mind during the highs and lows of manic depression. You will follow my anguished journey through a smorgasbord of psychiatric medications and psychological interventions. Come with me on the journey. Come with me on my path to recovery and learn how my journey continues drug free and asymptomatic of bipolar disorder.

Even if you are not personally affected by depression, bipolar disorder or anxiety, you will likely discover a little piece of yourself in my story. Much of what I cover throughout my narrative is universal and impacts all people in today's modern world. I've thrown in a little humor along the way to ease the burden of seriousness shrouding the topic of mental illness.

My mother and I coauthored *Meet Yourself in the Middle*, the result of which is a story told from two very different points of view: 1) my viewpoint from inside my bipolar nightmare; a personal account of what it's like to live with depression and mania, and 2) my mother's perspective as she watched me, her only daughter, decline into bipolar disorder and my associated suffering.

Depression in Modern Society

It is unlikely that any of us will escape the effects of depression. Even if we have not suffered from depression personally, we all know someone who has or who is still suffering from this mind-crippling plague. Approximately nineteen million Americans have been diagnosed with depression. Additionally there are many undiagnosed people who suffer in silence. I know of this from firsthand experience, as my father was just such a person. Search depression online, and close to ten million entries appear. These numbers, while staggering, are an indication of the epidemic of depression in modern society.

Many definitions of depression exist; however, it is basically a state of mind wherein one experiences a deep, unshakable sadness, and diminished interest in all activities and the outside world. Depression is formally diagnosed by the medical profession when a patient's morose feelings persist for more than two weeks preventing the patient from functioning in top form at work or socially. Doctors call this clinical or major depression. Psychiatry defines depression as a chemical imbalance in the brain that causes nerves in the brain to function improperly. My personal definition of depression is a complete lack of joy or worthiness in all areas of one's life.

Depression has become such a socially prevalent illness that millions of adults and children take antidepressants to manage symptoms of the disorder. Somehow it has become normal that people are unable to find joy and happiness in their lives. This physical experience we call life has reduced many to such tremendous amounts of pain and despair that they reach uncontrollably for numbing medication which, while a resource, is not the ultimate answer. In order to fully treat depression we must discover the root unhappiness and imbalance inside us to reach fulfillment and happiness. Such healing will provide longer-term contentment than medication ever will.

Healing Thyself

My experience shows that focusing attention on ways of avoiding and preventing the depression altogether is more productive than treating symptoms when they appear. For each individual, teachings, techniques and tools to achieve balance and happiness will be different. My story demonstrates the change that happens inside when you reach for joy, freedom and growth in your life.

Just as a dark room is void of light, depression is void of joy. In much the same way that you would eliminate the darkness of a room by flooding it with light, my story offers ways to eliminate the darkness of depression by flooding your mind with new thought patterns, bringing about a more harmonious way of living and feeling.

Telling My Story

Sooner or later we all have to come face to face with the question of who we are. We are not our body, we are not our mind, and we are not our emotions. So who are we? We are, in fact, much more than we can imagine. We are spiritual beings having a human experience, rather than human beings having a spiritual experience. When we begin to see beyond the world of form and into a realm of infinite possibilities we begin our long journey home. We wake up from our long slumber and start to heal our lives.

I consider myself to be a quick learner, yet I was pretty slow on the uptake to heed most of the lessons provided me during the dark period of my life! I have since found that the greatest gift of all lies in the darkness, and now offer this story to you.

Inside Bipolar Disorder

The very nature of bipolar disorder (also known as manic depression) is a paradox. Depression and mania are contradictory mental conditions. They are a complementary pair, showing up as major imbalances in the psyche. When a person is within normal range there seems to be a balance between the extremes. In my case the imbalance was so significant that it caused a flip from one end to the other resulting in extreme polarity. Mania feels amazing, euphoric and joyful. Depression feels heavy, dense, dark and painful.

Some say that mania occurs when a person is standing in both the physical and nonphysical dimensions of the universe at the same time. I can attest that manic feelings are blissful, joyful, omniscient, and omnipresent—a connection with all that is. I have since come to know that these manic qualities can best be described as a sense of ultimate knowing and awareness; however, words can express the actual feelings only in a much less dramatic way than what occurs during most manic episodes.

Depression is the ultimate misalignment with self. With depression the mind takes over and creates noise that keeps one stuck in a downward spiral of negative thinking. Nothing, and I mean nothing, inside depression is enjoyable. Instead, everything is lacking and painful, emotionally and physically. During my depressive episodes I felt as though I was surrounded by rolling black clouds of doom, completely hopeless and helpless.

Throughout my experiences with bipolar disorder, I talked continually about noise in my mind. In mania, these thoughts were fun and adventurous and gave me lots of energy, so much energy that I stopped sleeping for days. The noise manifests in one's mind and makes rapid-fire connections between events and people. Filters that we normally use to process the world disappear, and all data simultaneously and continuously enters the brain until the mania ends. Everything is much more intense, like drinking pure concentrated soda flavors without adding carbonated water. Mania causes a feeling of being totally connected to everyone and everything and is exciting and overwhelming at the same time.

The noise occurs quite differently in the depressed funk. Here it shows up as repeated circular thinking that is inescapable. It is like listening to a record that is stuck on a section of track that is full of negative words and energy. These negative thoughts attract other thoughts that are negative and the downward spiral continues. There is no sense of connection to current events. Everything appears as a memory with all the outcomes of the memories being pitiable. No one likes to hang around with the "neg head" in the crowd. Imagine realizing that the negative one is you and there is no escape! Sleep lets one escape for a time, but when one wakes up the negativity is waiting. There is no relief in sight, no reprieve, no hole in the noise for a smile, a joke or a song; just more of the same negative noise killing one's spirit, will and desire. The only real escape seems to be to take a vacation from oneself.

There are few personal accounts from inside the experience of bipolar disorder. Usually, anyone who has recovered will not want to recount their journey because it would be tantamount to reliving it. Even if someone wanted to recount their journey the internal chaos of the disorder renders it difficult to recall details of the experience. The illness itself impacts memory, recall and ability to see clearly. In addition, psychiatric drugs further impair function, making detailed accounts a scarcity.

When I felt myself tumbling into bipolar disorder, I did not consciously decide to write a book of my adventures. Unconsciously, though, I knew that I was embarking on a grave journey that I should document. I kept detailed journals during the five-year period of my bipolar episodes so I have a complete account of what actually happened and all of the nuances are available for me to share. While traveling through the chaos surrounding my descent into mental illness you will marvel at the miracle that allowed the journals to survive intact. Near the end of the book there are some of the actual pages taken from my journals. In addition, there are copies of some of the letters exchanged between my mother and me, shedding light on the darkest areas of my journey through madness. From these letters and journals, for myself and for the benefit of others affected by bipolar disorder I offer the following book.

A Journey Through Madness

Love enters as it leaves,
infinitesimal and yet -
the possibilities…

– PART I –

A Mother's Introduction

Anna was born on March 12, 1972, in a nursing home in Whitby, Yorkshire, attended by midwives. After dropping my son off at a friend's home, I drove myself to the nursing home just in time for tea with the nurses and midwives. Birth was less of a designer effort in those days, and was left in the hands of very competent nurses and midwives as doctors were not yet being paid to "catch babies." It was a very cold winter, the precursor to the "winter of discontent" of 1979 when we suffered through the coldest days, cooking and warming ourselves in front of the fireplace as, due to consistent labor unrest, electricity was only available for one or two hours a day. Perhaps the discontent was an omen of things to come in our personal lives. Anna's father did not come home for the birth of his daughter; he was working away and deemed the oil business more important than any family event. This single-parent design was a pattern that directed our destinies in ways that none of us could have imagined at the time.

Anna's depression developed over a long time span from late childhood through adolescence and into her young-adult years. During this time period, on numerous occasions I witnessed depression threaten my child's sanity and her will to live.

Growing Up
(1972 to 1995)

Even as young child I wondered why people had to live. I toyed with thoughts that dying would be easier. You see, I am one of those individuals who never felt like I belonged anywhere. I was a stranger to family, community and myself.

I was born in England. We moved three times and spent one year in South Africa all before I was four years old. At five, we moved from England to Texas and I spent my grade school years quiet and alone. I was terribly shy and had a difficult time adjusting to the customs and culture of the States. To cope with my feelings of being an "outsider," I was always a chameleon, adopting the style, language and habits of those within my social circle to better fit in.

When I entered junior high school, I decided to come out of my shell. I worked hard to make "friends" and soon became part of the popular crowd. My star rose quickly and my fiery fall was just as quick. For no good reason that I could see, I was kicked out of the group and onto the curb. Unmercifully and bewilderingly booted out of my safety net of friends, at twelve years of age I exploded into a fury, running in the opposite direction of my former crowd and deep into a social circle that was accepting of me. Or at least the "new" me. The me that fit with my new crowd.

I was preteen but my new friends were older, fifteen or sixteen. I changed my image from preppy to punk, shaved my head and wore flannels and boxers, long johns and Dr. Marten's boots. (One year I teased my hair into a Mohawk for school picture day and was left out of the yearbook because my "hair wasn't combed.") More destructive than our dubious fashion choices were our extra-curricular activities. Fairly harmless were our trips to the mall in roving packs designed to unsettle other patrons. Doing drugs and drinking alcohol were my new friends' favored activities, and became mine as well. We spent hours in teen clubs hanging out away from our parents and any adult authority. I spent days stoned or high, hiding it from my mother by staying out when she was in and remaining in my room if we found ourselves at home at the same time.

People What a Mess

"People What a Mess
People There Should Be Less
They're So Unkind
And They're Not Hard to Find
People What a Mess"

–Anna, Age Twelve

When I was thirteen years old, I attempted suicide twice, once with pills and once with a gun. After I locked myself in the bathroom and refused to come out, my mom intervened and took me to therapy. My first therapist maintained that all of my problems were the fault of my parents and, while that notion seemed attractive to consider, it did not help me heal. I next went to a hypnotherapist who was not much more helpful to me than my mother. I would sit in the office and talk, then get on the table and listen to a hypnosis tape, fall asleep, then wake up with a short-lived feeling of calm. Once a week for several months I continued to see the therapist. The hypnosis made my mind quiet, but only for a short time.

During the time when most children and teenagers rely on their parents to push back and provide structure, my family fell apart. When I was twelve my parents officially divorced, though my father had been gone for some time already. My mom cried all of the time. She worked constantly but could not make ends meet. There was nobody around for me except for my brother. Testosterone-fueled and seventeen, he made himself the "man of the house." I did not take lightly to his notions. The more he tried to manage me, the further my life spun out of control. Without a structure, I tumbled deeper and further into drugs. Under the psychedelic influence of LSD (acid) one of our group's favorite pastimes was to attend the midnight movies to see *The Wall*, (soundtrack by Pink Floyd) which illustrates a fall into madness. I can remember feeling deeply connected with the story at the time.

> *"If you should go skating*
> *On the thin ice of modern life*
> *Dragging behind you the silent reproach*
> *Of a million tear-stained eyes*
> *Don't be surprised when a crack in the ice*
> *Appears under your feet.*
> *You slip out of your depth and out of your mind*
> *With your fear flowing out behind you*
> *As you claw the thin ice."*
> —Waters, Pink Floyd, "The Wall"

Some of my friends were arrested on felony charges for LSD use and distribution, while others ended up in mental hospitals on so-called "bad trips." This is what happens when all the wonderment of hallucination turns sour and fear takes over in cruel and unusual ways. When I was fourteen, my internal voice finally told me to stop or I would be arrested and sent to prison or committed to a mental institution. The irony of this thought would be revealed several years later.

The only way for me to break the vicious cycle of drug abuse was to move. I left my mother's side and relocated from Texas to Derbyshire, England, to live with my father in the small village of Newcastle, and I had little in common with those of my age. My demons did not leave me. For eight years they lay mostly dormant, with only minor bouts of depression kicking at my heels. For eight years I hid my feelings well. While in high school in England I superbly acted the role of "normal," going to school, making decent grades and being "fine." At sixteen, I finished high school, went to college and earned the equivalent of an associate degree in business though I rarely went to class. I met Derek in Newcastle; he was five or six years older than I. We moved in together.

For several years I worked in various low-level marketing and temporary jobs. I learned to be a telemarketer. More importantly I learned how to be a corporate trainer. From all outside perspectives, I was doing well. I was all about success and achievement, using my skills and making a living. Despite the outward appearance of equilibrium, I would still wake up feeling empty and wonder what was the point, the worth of the daily grind? My lack of an internal mechanism to help maintain balance primed me for my first (mild) manic episode when I was twenty-one years old. From that high I crashed down, down, down into the darkest depths of depression and despair, and did not emerge for many long, dark and chaotic years.

Christmas 1994, Looming Problems

Christmas of 1994 a friend and I visited Anna and Derek in Newcastle. We stayed at Anna's business partner's home because their condo was too small to accommodate visitors. By all appearances Anna and Derek shared a happy home but there were hints, even then, that I should have realized meant more serious problems were ahead. I had always suspected that Anna used too many recreational drugs, a carry over from her teenage years. My partner at the time recognized some of the underlying hints as he was closer to the drug scene because he taught on a college level. Apparently Anna was using marijuana on a regular basis. I chose to ignore this and believe it was none of my business. I also knew that Derek had an aversion to marriage. I suspected that Anna was not happy about this and might view it as rejection. Their finances were also suspect at the time. It was not apparent how they could afford a condo, two cars and their hectic lifestyle in Newcastle where everything cost double that of any city in the States.

Anna and Derek entertained us royally and, to my later regret, I never broached any of the potential problems that were looming on the horizon. Our family as a whole never liked to discuss problems before they were out of hand. This has proved to be one of our greatest failings.

Roller Coaster

I first glimpsed mania after attending a self-discovery workshop, designed to tear down and rebuild participants' view of the world and partially forces that change by imposing an unknown schedule, sleep deprivation, prolonged periods of sitting in uncomfortable places, and few and unscheduled breaks. The goal of the workshops is to inspire individuals to jump their personal hurdles and conquer the world.

While at the workshop, lack of sleep, food, and constant conditioning threw off track the little sense of balance remaining in my system. From constant indoctrination about my own power and responsibility to control my destiny, I left the workshop on the wings of possibility. I believed I had learned secrets to the very meaning of success and life! At the time I did not think it unusual that I would experience a prolonged heightened sense of euphoria. I was high on life, invincible. I was "Walkin' on Sunshine." I was excited! I could do anything! I knew the secret to success and was ready to apply it to my life—immediately!

The day after returning from the workshop I was ready to take on the world alone, so I quit my job and started my own consulting practice. As a parting gift, my employer let me take over part of his company's training practice. I had no plan and no money, but I forged ahead. The self-discovery workshop teaches powerful lessons about personal experience and sources of happiness. However, without a stable internal compass, the workshop unseated my soul— badly. I had no relationship with my internal self and had not the faintest idea of how to apply the principles I learned in any way but externally. What goes up must come down, and two weeks later I crashed and slid into despair.

I had always hidden my innermost thoughts and feelings, acting on the outside the way it seemed I should. Even after the workshop I continually strived to achieve success by outward appearances only. Inside I was still deeply lost and confused, with no idea how to help myself. I had learned from my father "Never, ever let them know what you're feeling inside. Just smile and carry on." I really took this to heart. It became my mantra. In order to keep up appearances, I acted as if I felt okay. I believed that letting people know what was really going on inside me would give them information to be used against me later. As my business grew, the disconnect between my inner feelings and my external actions became more disruptive in my life.

Inside I felt like a fraud. I trained top one hundred United Kingdom businesses on improving customer service and performance. I enthusiastically sold business managers and company presidents on the merits of this or that, while inside I felt like a wet, smelly dishrag, of no help to anyone. To bolster my confidence, I found a business partner. She was twenty years older than I and I needed her experience to manage the money side of the business. Unfortunately, she was a taker, not a giver. Manipulative and calculating, she managed "our" business for her own benefit. With no self esteem, I had no ability to react as she used guilt to leverage our situation to her advantage. For "us," but really for her, I went without pay for months, supporting her while she divorced her husband and became a single mother. Though supposedly equal partners in business, her rationale was that I had a life-partner who could support me and, therefore, I did not need the money. In my mind, that made sense. I felt deserving of nothing anyway.

I took a trip to London, alone, to visit my dad. There I met Colin. Immediately, in my mind, sparks flew. He was gorgeous and charming, and I was instantly sucked into an affair. Methodical and logical, deliberate and steady, he was the complete opposite of me. Around Colin I felt high on our chemistry together, a stark contrast to my depression. I returned home from London, my brain a tortured mess.

Though I hadn't physically interacted with Colin, I still felt unfaithful to Derek. Despite my loyalty to him, inside I knew my relationship with Derek was not working. Unsure of our destiny together and wanting more commitment, I sat him down and asked him where we were headed and would he marry me. I intentionally created a situation in which he had to choose whether we would be together or separate. (Later I would find Derek was one of the few who really had my best interests at heart.)

While Derek deliberated, I met Colin for a weekend at a seaside resort and consummated our affair. Upon returning home, I confessed everything. Derek and I separated and I found my own apartment.

I got lost in my new love. Colin, my Mr. Wonderful, was a perfect diversion; a great escape from my unwanted life. Kind and generous, he showered me with attention. Our chemistry and sex was amazing. With Colin, for the first time, I felt awake to all facets of being a woman. It was like a dream. I soared to new heights of euphoria and I wanted it to last forever. Most likely, outsiders assumed I was high on life and love. I was on a roller coaster of ups and downs but none were yet so frightening that I had to shut my eyes. My mood swings, while not necessarily fun, were at that point still bearable.

Crash Landing
Newcastle, England
(October 1995 to March 1996)

Depression feels no different after one is formally diagnosed. Attaching a name to my illness did not help me feel better. "Depression hurts" is a mild descriptor for the emotional torture that crushes the human psyche. I felt like my head was in a vice and any stimulation cranked the vice tighter. The only safe place was to sit, numb in bed or catatonic on the couch. The simplest things—getting dressed or washing a few dishes—were beyond me.

We lost our office and my business partner and I moved our center of operations to my small apartment. I would go into my home office and try to work, but creating ideas was beyond my reach. I could not think, plan, type; I could no longer function. My mind was broken. To me, a cognitive and analytical person, a broken mind was a fate worse than death. A life without a functioning mind was no life at all.

At 3:20 A.M. the clank of the milk bottles being delivered sent a rush of dread through my veins. Another night spent lying awake wondering when the nightmare would stop. The thoughts didn't make any sense yet they persisted. What will I do? What can I do? I can't do anything. I am useless and weak. Where am I? What happened to me? Why can't I do anything? Sleep was the only escape from these thoughts, yet sleep wouldn't come.

The alarm blared at 7 A.M. I still had not slept, not a wink at all. I would spend another day alone in the flat with nothing more to do than to recount the endless bills that were piling up on the floor or the stacks of dishes overflowing in the kitchen. The sound of people busy about their day deafened me. Even the television could not hold my attention. I was barely able to hear it above the noise inside my head. Do something you useless bag of shit. Get off your ass and get on with this life. You can't kill yourself; you're too chicken for that so get on with it. Sitting here and doing nothing is not the right answer. Yet I was paralyzed. Any activity was too difficult for me. The hours, oh the hours, they were never ending.

During this time I was loved and I was not alone, but I was unable to reach anyone. My inability to communicate and close associates' inability to understand what they were seeing caused them to remain out of reach, as if on the other side of a glass wall. One day I sat in the bathtub, crying. Thoughts of despair raced through my head: They'd be better off without me. What will become of me? Will I sit here long enough that I become catatonic? Will someone else put me out of my misery? Will I wake up tomorrow and find that this was all a bad dream? Please, God, anything but this. The pain is overwhelming me. Maybe tomorrow it will be better. Maybe tomorrow I will be able to go outside and stand in the sunshine.

Colin and my business partner chose this time to talk to me about the business. They did not realize that any conversation outside how I would put one foot in front of the other was beyond my reach. While trying to listen to them I finally realized that, just as I did not know what to do with myself, they had no idea what to do either. They made vague attempts to maintain business as usual but both my boyfriend and my business partner were totally freaked out. They had no idea how to handle what was going on with me. I knew it, they knew it—but we never talked about it. I remember being angry, listening to them chat on the couch, smoking and laughing, while I was locked in my own mind, unable to get out. Our apartment was tiny and I had no privacy, further aggravating my situation.

Outside stimulation and interaction with people tightened the already unbearable squeeze on my head, so I stopped leaving the apartment. I sat with the lights off, smoking and drinking coffee, alone in my head. This went on for weeks. If I chose to summon enough energy to interact with him, Colin would listen to my ramblings and cook and clean for me. For a while he tried to help me in what small ways that he could as he continued working.

Staying in did not heal my head. Lack of privacy combined with my chaos of thoughts overwhelmed me. I had to get away. I wanted to be alone, to disappear, and there was no possibility of doing that at home. I waited until no one was looking and, like a child sneaking out, I slipped out my front door and began walking. Barely conscious, I stepped out to cross the street and completely missed seeing an approaching vehicle that nearly mowed me down. A nearby stranger pulled me back and saved me from being hit. Although my misstep had been unintentional, I did consider the idea that being run over would have made for an easy way out. I have heard people talk about having medicine head, being drugged with everything hazy around the edges. I had depression head, fuzzy and deeply isolating. I was so far within my own mind that my senses did not work. My soul was lost, and without that, I had no direction, no compass, no balance. I was a pendulum on an unbalanced clock, swinging unevenly with no rhythm, out of time. When I started walking, I didn't really have a purpose other than removing myself from my current situation to make the suffering stop.

After practically sleepwalking for almost two miles, I found myself at Derek's apartment. Derek answered my knock, very surprised to see me. We had barely spoken for a year. Crying hysterically and uncontrollably, I asked him if he would be willing to do one last favor for me. I pleaded with him not to deny my request: I begged him to help me die. Even with our rocky history together, my infidelity, and our failed relationship, Derek still cared for me. He held me tightly as I sobbed. Eventually I fell asleep. I don't know how long I stayed; perhaps it was several hours. Derek contacted Colin to let him know I was safe, and later drove me home. He also called my mom to let her know I was in serious trouble and needed her. Later that night, I learned that she was on her way from Canada to get me. When Derek opened the door to me that afternoon, he saw a skinny, sad and exhausted woman, a shadow of the person with whom he had shared part of his life. Over the several months since we'd split up and my so-called Mr. Wonderful had entered my life, I had lost everything. Derek knew me well, and with one look he understood that something was terribly wrong. His loving and caring nature led him to intervene as nobody had previously been able. I do not know if Derek knows what a gift he was to me the day. He saved my life.

A Daughter in Trouble

After several phone conversations with Derek and Anna, I knew that Anna was in trouble and once again my help was required in England. The timing was very difficult for me. I was about to write my finals for my bachelor of science in nursing. I made arrangements to postpone my exams until the next session and boarded a plane for Newcastle. I found my daughter in dire straights healthwise, personally and financially.

Anna was now living with Colin in a house they had rented for a price far beyond their means. Colin, a plumber by trade, a man with little ambition and a penchant for living off women, was well entrenched in Anna's life. He interfered with her business, her business partner and her friends. By this time they had borrowed money from Anna's friends and were continuing to use a friend's credit card. Anna had run her own cards up to the limit and Colin had no credit. They were busily creating a mire of debt that no one could correct.

I made arrangements to meet with the landlord at Anna's place of business and found that they owed approximately five thousand pounds sterling for their office space and sundries. The landlord was very worried about Anna as he had watched as she dropped about twenty pounds and became less available at the workplace. He informed me that Anna's partner was not professional and did not seem to pull her weight. I took a look at the books and discovered that the only business her partner was conducting was entirely personal, such as e-mails to her latest boyfriend. The business partner was never available for consultation with me although she and Colin had determined that if only I would loan them some more money they would be able to turn the business around. *Knowing that the business had been built and managed by Anna, and seeing Anna struggle to get out of bed, I knew that there could be no salvation as long as Anna remained ill.*

Anna was indeed ill. She would lie in bed for hours but remained unable to sleep and continued to worry herself into a frenzy about what she was going to do. The house was a mess; laundry and clothes everywhere, the kitchen a disaster. When I attempted to discuss the problems with Colin, he was resistant and belligerent, and disagreed with all suggestions. During my stay he disappeared most nights, spending them at the home of Anna's business partner. In the end I knew the only deliverance for my daughter was to get her away from these people, so I arranged for Anna to return with me to Canada. Colin and Anna's business partner met this plan with much resistance, as both realized that Anna's departure meant the end of the money train.

Five Months and Five Cities
(April 1996 to August 1996)

I don't know how I ended up agreeing to go with my mother to Canada. Every thought in my head had two conflicting sides. On one hand, I believed that by leaving the situation, I would get better. On the other hand, I thought I needed to stay and face things. Before I knew it, though, my bags were packed and we left for Canada.

I was consumed with stress and panic throughout the entire trip. Every time we changed location I had a panic attack, and would freeze, unable to move forward. My mom had to coax me all the way to her apartment in Kelowna, British Columbia. Upon our arrival she did everything she could to help me. She provided my favorite foods to eat, arranged for medical attention and introduced me to interesting people. She gave me space and privacy to do whatever I wanted. All with the idea that she could reach through the glass box cutting me off from the world. Just as no one else could, my mom could not cure my depression with still more outside stimulation. Nor could she break my internal cycle of negative thoughts. Thousands of miles away from the problems I left in England, I was in purgatory. Unable to get well, but not getting worse, I remained in a stasis of depression and despair.

I did seek medical help during this period, and met with a revolving door of psychiatrists and psychotherapists. While not believing or trusting any of them I tried to listen and heed their advice but in the end I could not.

Kelowna, British Columbia

Anna and I were back in Kelowna, sharing an apartment with an old school friend of mine who showed a great deal of compassion and patience while we attempted to work through Anna's depression. In addition to taking care of a daughter with depression, I continued with my final few months of study and practicum to complete my nursing degree, all the while working two jobs to manage financially. Stress did not stop there; my son was getting married in New York and this was the next trip on our agenda.

During this time period I had several people attempt to speak with Anna in private, asking for no explanations after the fact. I don't think anyone managed to get through to Anna. Her mind was set on returning to Newcastle ,where she believed her true friends and a life awaited her. In the interim, Derek was attending an HIV conference in Vancouver and made the trip to Kelowna to see Anna. It was apparent that Derek still cared for Anna and that he some-how harbored feelings of guilt for not having seen after her better in England. Anna and Derek visited for a few days and she decided to return with him to England—and Colin. But Anna was unable to get on the plane in Vancouver and Derek brought her back to Kelowna. Now she was out of options. I was not about to fund another ticket and she had no money. I tried to get Anna to see that there was a reason for her mind and body refusing to get on the plane to England, but even this did not deter her desire to return to Colin. She was like a person possessed.

All during this period Colin continued to call and upset her on a daily basis.

This caused endless unrest in our small household, along with feelings of rage and helplessness. He was persistent in wanting her back in England. I think he felt his meal ticket slipping away forever. Although Anna was no longer capable of working or caring for herself, he knew that friends and family would continue to ensure that she remained in a viable situation. Eventually Colin came up with the money to purchase Anna another ticket to England, financed with her friend Tara's credit card. Anna, determined to return to the center of chaos, left Kelowna once again and returned to England to be with Colin. She also wanted to be near her father and stepmother, with whom Colin had remained friends. The true evil of that relationship remained to be realized.

Three Months of Travel

My mom and I traveled to New York for my brother's wedding, then on to Houston while she sat for her state nursing exams, and subsequently back to Kelowna. While constantly traveling, I conveniently focused on my changing surroundings, hoping my situation would resolve itself. My attention was never on getting well, just about moving on.

Although I agreed to the travel, I was miserable and anxiety filled. Depression rendered me devoid of energy and unable to communicate well. I was consumed with the notion that I did not want to bother anyone. I was trying to be happy but felt I was ruining every new situation into which I entered.

My brother's wedding was a horrendous start to our journey. Darren was marrying a Puerto Rican girl with a huge family. Mom and I were used to our small family wherein quiet and calm were the norm. I became like a drunk on a merry-go-round, struggling through a whirlwind of days full of boisterous relatives. My continual need to act happy made my head ache. Being surrounded by unfamiliar people was painful and agonizing. For three months as we traveled, I tried, summoning every ounce of energy, to smile, stay calm and not cause trouble. Acting happy became my punishment. Having been deeply depressed for over six months, I was resigned to the fact that my life would always be difficult and painful and this was what I deserved. There remained nothing to live for and nothing to die for; just an empty life with occasions for acting out happiness I would never feel again. This was in stark contrast to what I had learned during my self-discovery workshop, where I was told I could conquer the world and live happily ever after.

When Mom and I were back in Kelowna I began to make plans to return to Newcastle where the pain had all begun. I felt that I needed to go back and close the loop on the life I had left hanging. I was alone in my mind, attempting to make decisions to resolve my situation, but I had no idea what resolution meant.

Returning to Newcastle
(August 1996 to November 1996)

I went back to a new but bitter world. My best friend had moved on while I was away. So had my business partner, taking the remaining business, our new car and all of our clients with her. She "generously" offered me a job at her "new" company. I was lucid enough to realize that was not an option.

I had no money; just a pile of bills. I decided to file bankruptcy. Arriving at this decision was much more difficult than the actual process. I filed papers, went to court and stood in front of a judge. The smack of the gavel and the stamp on the paper declaring me officially bankrupt echoed through my head. Though bankruptcy signified only a lack of money, to me it signaled complete nakedness. At twenty-five years old, I once again was arriving in the world naked. I stood in the courtroom feeling stripped and exposed. I had only one choice—rebuild my life. This would be a monumental task, bankruptcy being far more serious in England than in the U.S.A.

For eight months I lay in bed, rising and going out only for small intervals. I didn't notice it at the time but sleep was a great healer. All the rest from sleeping sixteen hours a day restored my mind somewhat. My days were not so torturous and the mind noise seemed quieter. I was still very shaky, but for the first time in months I could see, hear and process events going on around me. I had lost all my confidence, but realized I had to start again: one day, one hour, one minute at a time.

Shortly after my return to Newcastle, Colin proposed to me and I accepted. Once we set a date for the wedding, I giddily started planning. It gave me something to look forward to. I began to act like a bride: buying wedding planners and magazines, planning parties, and giggling with girlfriends. These were nice, normal activities for me. Feeling "normal" was rare and I was grateful.

I secured a position managing a hotel, owned by friends, in Northumberland. They needed an on-site manager, which was perfect for Colin and meant we would be provided both housing and income. We packed our bags and moved to the country. The work was hard and the hours were long, but I felt great! I loved my new role managing the hotel and socializing with the guests. I felt lucky to have emerged so far from the darkness. Nothing could have prepared me for what came next: The darkest chapter of my life was yet to unfold.

Feeling Good Now, Hadrian's Lodge, Northumberland
(November 1996 to July 1997)

Hadrian's Lodge was on a twenty-five-acre property with its buildings arranged in a square courtyard; fourteen rooms in one building, a restaurant in another, owner's quarters on one side, and four holiday cottages on the other. It was built near Hadrian's Wall and, according to legend, upon ancient burial grounds. Set amidst endless rolling hills of grass, the property had lakes where the builder's children purportedly drowned. Every morning and evening, fog would roll in and over the lakes, cloaking the landscape in eerie quiet. With gloomy ghost stories and wind sweeping over the hills and through our passageways, the hotel's construction provided some mind-boggling moments.

Running a hotel, though entertaining, is a draining twenty-four-hour, seven-day-a-week job. I was the front-of-house manager and receptionist. Colin was the cook and did the cleaning. I rarely slept more than a few hours, but I had no choice. The work had to be done and, wish though we did, there were no other staff members to ease our burden.

The lodge's heating was almost non-existent and the kitchen supporting the restaurant was no more than an ordinary household kitchen, not quite up to the task of meal preparation for hotel guests. The work produced very stressful situations and required ingenuity and charm. Sometimes it descended into sheer panic. For example, the stay of a group from a school for the blind induced endless chaos. On another occasion, the restaurant associated with the hotel was shuttered by the health department in the middle of a bachelor party.

Every area of our jobs was labor-intensive and mentally demanding. Constant pressure to be social, run the hotel and restaurant and plan my wedding wound my brain up like a set of snapping teeth. I was upbeat and cheerful one moment and erupted like a volcano the next. I careened around, working, planning and worrying, never stopping for a minute.

The wedding would be tricky as my father and mother would be obliged to be together for the first time in years. My stepmother, Nancy, had the creepy habit of constantly talking to others about my childhood. She regaled people with stories of my pets and my life when my parents were still together, insinuating that she had always hovered around my life like a ghost. Although she and my father had engaged in an affair during my parents' marriage, Nancy was a latecomer in our lives. In addition, my mother disapproved of Colin. I imagined this "family reunion" would be something like *The Big Chill*. I felt responsible for everyone else's happiness, since I could never be sure my own.

Amidst the nonstop work and wedding plans, I tended bar in the hotel pub. On one occasion a drama society was visiting; just the type of people with whom I normally felt a connection. A guest asked how someone like me came to be in a place like that. He was probably making small talk in a guest lodge on the edge of civilization. In my hyperactive state, I felt that he saw deep into my psyche, what I hid from the rest of the world. I envisioned super-connectedness to this person in a way that I had never felt before. This person could somehow see me, as nobody else could. I was overwhelmed; the air around me was suddenly intoxicating. I was alive. I was new. I was understood and I had new understanding of the world, understanding that had eluded me for years. In a burst of pure euphoria, I ran from the pub to my private quarters to share the experience with my fiancé.

My retelling of this revelation made Colin angry. Looking back, I think I had been acting strange for some time though in a different way than my previous depression. At the time, all I knew was that I was feeling GREAT and it seemed incomprehensible to me that someone who loved me would not fully support my feelings. I was having the best day of my life and all Colin could do was frown upon it.

After Colin's reaction to my experience in the bar, I wondered if he was on my side. I began to see him as the enemy. I believed he would steal my newly found enlightenment and force me back into the box of living like everyone else. So I began to protect myself, doing things like barricading myself in the bedroom, which just made him break down the door. Somehow he was able to penetrate my paranoia and convince me that his motives were true and genuine. I fixated on rooting out the true enemies to my newfound happiness. I kept asking "Where are my reinforcements? I need troops here to help me hold onto my new found euphoria and protect it at any cost." I had become enlightened and I experienced everything around me with expanded consciousness. I had newly found secrets to encompass the universe, had the secret of true knowing, and was connected to everyone and everything. I could see past what normal people could: I could see beneath the surface, beyond the realm of others, and was empowered with the gift of sight, a vision of souls and nature. My powers were magical, mystical and energizing. I had become, I had realized my potential. I no longer required sleep because I had surpassed the need for such mortal things. I was free. Inside my head, the noise grew louder. Everything I experienced was concentrated. My senses were magnified and everything looked more colorful, sounded more intense, smelled stronger, felt more powerful. Every time I touched something I received an electric shock. Hadrian's Lodge was near a large electrical power plant, and I had harnessed its energy. Even my speaking voice sounded electrified.

During moments of great clarity, I did know that I was walking a thin line between sanity and insanity (Well, perhaps it had been muted). I recall telling Colin that I had discovered the portal that would allow me to explore what it was like to be out of one's mind for a while and then come back. If I was able to sleep long enough, eat nutritious food, and find myself grounded I could always come back. Eventually, though, the insanity and the mania took over.

One night, after gaining the keys to eternal bliss and happiness, I called my father. His life was a trainwreck. He had spent time in prison because of fraud. He was an alcoholic, smoked constantly and had emphysema. His voice was hoarse and he told me he was dying. He always said he was dying; however, in my mania, I took his words at face value, believing that he was in fact dying and would be dead before my wedding day. Because of our similar personalities and madness, I had always believed that we had a connection beyond that of father/daughter. I would experience knowing when he was in trouble or needed help. I always thought, in the back of my mind, that I was destined to have a life like his—which would be a life not worth living—and because I shared his genes I would have no choice. After our phone call, I got dressed, picked up my car keys, intending to drive to London, more than five hours away, in the middle of the night. Colin stopped me and I flew into a rage, threw my keys at Colin, missed and broke a mirror. During my manic phases, my emotions were on a hair trigger, and I would fly from from bliss to terror to rage and back with alarming speed and frequency.

Eventually the hotel owners hired a man to run the hotel while I planned my wedding. I think at this point they suspected something else was not quite right with me; however, no one intervened. Steven, the newly hired manager, was unaware of the baby monitors at reception and would spend each night on the telephone speaking long-distance to Japan. I frequently told him I knew what he was up to, but by this time—although I really did know what was going on—no one believed me.

I began to communicate with those around me through song lyrics. Tori Amos' words from "Silent All These Years" and "Happy Phantom" frequently became my preferred method of expression. Words from "Happy Phantom" —"If I die today I'll be the happy phantom and I'll go chasing the nuns out in the yard"— were eventually the last straw for my family and convinced them I needed help. While I thought I wasn't feeling suicidal at all and was feeling better than I had ever felt in my entire life, I must have eventually gotten tired. My mom tells me that when she and my brother arrived at Hadrian's Lodge, the first words out of my mouth were "Thank God the reinforcements have arrived. I can sleep now." And sleep I did for a short while.

The Dark Side of Mania

Hadrian's Lodge, situated in a bleak part of Northumberland, stands open to the wind lonely in a pasture of undulating mist. It is a modern-day architectural disaster and reminded me of the tenements built across the country during the nineteen sixties. A true "Bleak" house, stone and slate, low to the ground, as if cowering from the harsh landscape.

All of these thoughts went through my head as I drove up the winding road towards Hadrian's Lodge. I had just arrived from Canada with jet lag and the sense of being hopelessly lost my only companions. It was early in the week and my daughter was to be married in a couple of days. My son, Darren, and his new wife, Yvette, were already in residence. It was they who had provided me with the meager directions I had to reach Hadrian's Lodge. I stopped periodically to call on my journey from London and they gave measured warnings about what I was about to encounter. Little did I know the heartbreaking circumstances that we all would face in the coming weeks and months.

On arrival at Hadrian's Lodge my son and daughter-in-law welcomed me and took me to a small and very cold bedroom and cautioned what I could expect upon seeing Anna. Even though they had tried to prepare me for the chaos I encountered in Anna and Colin's living quarters, I was astounded. The place was a tip, trash abounded, dirty clothes every where, Anna was dancing on the bed, music from both radio and stereo spewing forth a cacophony of noise that seemed to be competing for residence in Anna's world. The greeting from my daughter was, "Thank God the reinforcements have arrived." I had little experience with drugs on a personal level but my professional mind ensured me that what I was witnessing was a very bad trip of unknown origin. But I didn't anticipate the journey that would continue to haunt us for years.

As Anna will tell you, she thought she was invincible and that everything she was doing was beyond our understanding. In that respect she was correct. None of us understood how to help. The one person who had a handle on what was happening or had caused this break with reality was Colin, the Evil C as he eventually became known.

Colin was Anna's fiancé, a pretty boy who had made a career of living off women. We had met Colin previously when we all shared a Christmas celebration in New York, shortly after Darren and Yvette were married. Anna had financed his trip to New York, their shopping, and New Years Eve in Times Square all charged to my credit cards. Using other people's credit cards was a staple of Colin's insatiable thirst for the good life he felt was his privilege. There was also a hint of the unfaithful which was brought to my attention in a cock-and-bull story about his being hired to employ his magic plumbing skills for some wealthy women in the U.S. I felt at the time that Colin was a predator, but when someone is in love/lust there is nothing you can do to persuade them that their partner may be less than ideal.

I decided to get Anna away from the noise and she came to my room briefly to look at some things I had brought her for the wedding. She was distracted and when I asked to see her wedding dress she seemed confused and looked at me strangely. I do not think that she knew where the dress was nor do I feel that she realized none of us could afford to pay for it. I recall her describing it to me on the phone several weeks preceding the wedding and I thought at the time that it sounded very grandiose. I couldn't glean much information from Anna about wedding plans but was led to believe that Nancy, my ex-husband's wife, had been helping. I called Nancy and Ross and was amazed to discover that they might not even be up to attending the wedding and they knew nothing about plans. I also described how Anna was and asked if they knew of her apparent ill health—they of course claimed ignorance, a state I attributed as normal within that group.

The second indication that things were going to get much worse was a negative encounter with Colin. Anna was having a long soak in the bath and she had invited me to come and talk with her while she rested. I thought this might be an opportunity to get some answers so I went along and sat in the steamy room and listened while she attempted to make normal conversation. By this time Anna was having difficulty concentrating and completing thoughts. Her sentences where disjointed and unfinished, and she lurched from one subject to another. She was just beginning to relax when Colin came into the bathroom with a cup of tea and a joint for Anna. I begged him not to give her any drugs. Little did I know that this had been going on for some time. I still don't know what all she had been given and when. Colin told me that joints were good for her and helped her relax. He also made it quite clear that the drug issue was none of my business. By the next morning Anna was almost catatonic, and I attempted to talk her into seeing a doctor. Colin was very against this and I left to let her sleep off the effects of the drugs. I think Anna may have slept little again that night, but in the next morning when I went to find them they were both sound asleep. I wondered how it was that they could get away with sleeping late when they were supposed to be managing the hotel. Hadrian's Lodge advertised bed and breakfast and it had been Colin's job to cook breakfast for the guests. There was no breakfast that morning and only they knew how many previous breakfasts had been missed.

By now I was scared and wanted nothing more than to get my daughter to a doctor to get some help for whatever was going on. Colin told me to get out of their room and leave Anna alone. I was afraid and attempted to call the ambulance service but I had no idea how to direct the ambulance to the lodge and Colin wouldn't help me. He threatened to throw me out of the property and the day got progressively worse. Finally, through deception, my son and daughter-in-law and I got Anna into the car and took her to a doctor in the local village. During our visit with the doctor Anna became very angry, stamping her feet, rushing around in the office. She was unable to speak clearly but she came out

with all manner of curses and diatribes against me and her brother for bring-
ing her to the doctor. The doctor spent only fifteen minutes listening to this and
then he called the psychiatric unit and asked for an emergency admission. A
seventy-two-hour hold order was put in place and Anna's nightmare began in
earnest.

Seventy-two-hour Hold
Newcastle
(July 1997)

"Look how white everything is, how quiet, how snowed-in
I am learning peacefulness, lying by myself quietly
As the light lies on these white walls, this bed, these hands.
I am nobody; I have nothing to do with explosions.
I have given my name and my day-clothes up to the nurses
And my history to the anesthetist and my body to surgeons"

–Sylvia Plath, "Tulips"

I stood on the street corner waiting for my mom and brother to pull the car around. This is the same corner on which I stood after leaving the doctor's office with my diagnosis of clinical depression. I do not remember anyone standing with me, but there must have been somebody, or else I would have just wandered off. Whoever stood with me did not register. I felt completely alone again.

We went to the hospital. I was still under the impression that I was going to visit my "dying" dad. My phone conversation with him had planted enough worry in my mind to make it seem plausible that we were on the way to visit him, not to visit another psychiatrist for me. My dad also lived hundreds of kilometers away from where we were, but during this phase I had no concept of time or space. Everything was one long continuum of misery.

Imagine my surprise, then, when I did not find my dad at the hospital, but was ushered into yet another doctor's office. Furious with my mother, brother and everyone around me, I immediately reached for my crutch, a cigarette, which they told me to put out because we were in a hospital. Literally and completely out of my mind, I again asked for a cigarette, then looked down and saw that I already held one in my hand. I realized, at that moment how crazy I must have appeared to everyone around me. I realized, finally, that there was no way for me to talk myself out of that room, out of yet another diagnoses or out of whatever their plans for me would be. I remember nothing else until I woke in the hospital, three days later.

It was the middle of the night, and I was in an unfamiliar place. I had no idea how long I had been sleeping or where I was. My first thought was "I really need a cigarette." I cracked open the door to an empty corridor with a light at one end and a waft of stale cigarette smoke coming from the other. I crept out of my room and followed my nose and the sound of a television blaring at the end of the hall.

I entered what appeared to be a day room. The TV was mounted up high where no one could adjust the channel or volume. The table underneath the television was strewn with magazines from a time and place quite different than the present. Cheap plastic chairs lined the walls on all sides. In the corner sat a strange skinny little man wearing a baseball cap and puffing on a cigarette. He offered me one, which I gladly accepted. We sat without talking for a minute or two, then the strange man spoke, "What are you in for?" "Excuse me?" I replied. "Who's on first?" said the man. "What's on second?" He began to laugh hysterically. I learned throughout the next few weeks that reciting the old Abbot and Costello routine was how he passed the time. However, here, in the middle of the night, not knowing where I was and listening to his strange ramblings was quite terrifying. I quickly smoked my cigarette, stubbed it out and fled back to my room.

In that room, the only clues to my whereabouts were an untouched glass of water with a bendable "sippy" straw and a document titled "Section 42." My wedding was supposed to be happening (Had it already happened?). Instead I was dumped here, wherever "here" was. I sat on the bed and began to read "Section 42." The words slammed me full force: "You have been sectioned under the Mental Health Act for 28 days. During this time you will remain hospitalized for continuous observation." With that document I learned the meaning of being "held against one's will." My worst fears had been realized. I was locked up in a mental institution. I thought "Oh God what has happened to me? How will I get out?" Then I became furious with everyone. I was stuck here because of my family. They had betrayed me.

Mental hospitals are somewhat like prisons, perhaps a little more colorful. The mental ward of Newcastle Infirmary was bizarre and chaotic—a zoo of lost souls. Every day one of the inmates would have an outburst that would scare the pants off of everyone, including the staff. When I first arrived at the hospital I was on the ground floor in a low-security private room. Although we were all supposedly hospitalized to keep ourselves "safe," I never felt secure. Every patient had his or her own demons to fight, some had frequent violent outbursts. Doctors, nurses and orderlies tried to maintain order, mainly through sedation. According to the psychiatrists, while each patient had their unique problems, these could all be solved with medications. Authoritarian nurses provided, and then enforced, the medication regimes with the ever-hovering aura of possible retaliation for sins yet uncommitted. Orderlies tried to be nice and helpful but had no real say in our care. They gave us crayons to write with and out-of-date newspapers and magazines to read. We were bored out of what little mind we had left! We were a simmering soup of unsettled souls with very few people keeping order.

The wide variety of ailments and personalities thrown together ensured a constant air of instability. I later discovered that the man I met when I first woke was a schizophrenic named John. He liked to recite the old baseball joke of who's on first, what's on second all day long. He always had a smile on his face and was welcoming. Not everyone was so friendly. Linda-the fire-starter was in because of a psychotic break of some kind. She carried a lighter with her everywhere she went and threatened to light one on fire if one didn't pay attention to her. She was always in everyone face, invading what little personal space we were afforded. Linda was allowed to have her lighter (against all common sense) because her medications left her hands so shaky that she could not keep it lit long enough to do any damage.

Even though we were locked up, our personal items were not and we could never be certain that everything would remain in its place once we left our room. One man liked to collect shoes. He wandered from room to room, always taking only one of each pair of shoes he could find. Later the orderlies would find piles of shoes under his bed, under his covers or under his pillow. Subsequently, we all walked around with mismatched shoes after one of his rounds. Thinking back, the idea that it was like being in the movie *One Flew over the Cuckoo's Nest* seems appropriate. Such movies exaggerate less than we would like to think, in particular regarding medications and sedation. For example, immediately upon my arrival in Newcastle Infirmary, I was started on rounds of medication, beginning with lithium. (It is also used in batteries.) Lithium plus the other medications I was on were so mind numbing that I can only recall fragments of what happened during the month I was incarcerated.

The food was horrendous. In between meals all we had to snack on were crackers, peanut butter and packets of jelly. I constantly asked for food, like a hamburger, from the outside. There was no rehabilitation or therapy available. The picture of mental patients passing time at a crafts table is completely accurate. I still have a fake-stained-glass project from my time in the hospital. (Real glass would have been dangerous for mental patients.)

After the first week, which I spent mostly in a daze, I recall psychiatrists and psychologists stopping by to talk to me, asking the same questions over and over again. I found this very aggravating and shouted them out of my room on more than one occasion, which probably interfered later with my pleas to be released. The idea that a mental hospital is meant to provide an atmosphere conducive to healing is fantasy. The destabilizing effects of volatile wardmates and constant unannounced changes in treatment did not nor cannot allow wellness. There is no calm in a mental hospital. Everyone is constantly on edge. Some patients had daily treatments of electroshock therapy. We could hear them screaming down the hallway. The threat of shock therapy or simply being constrained to a bed was enough to keep most of us in line.

Rather than even trying to get well, I focused on how to get out. I constantly called family members and begged them to come get me. However, once placed on a legal hold it is the doctors who have the power to release a patient regardless of the patient's or family's wishes.

I passed the time sleeping and writing in my journal. Visiting hours, smoke breaks and meal times were the highlights of my days. While still undiagnosed I was put on different medications to see how I would react. My reactions to the drugs would eventually lead to my diagnosis. I endured terrible side effects: swollen tongue, slurred speech, hand tremors, dry mouth, thrush, and chronic drowsiness were a few.

Visiting Hours on the Ward

I do not believe there are enough words to describe the feelings I had when first I was allowed to see my daughter in the psychiatric unit at the Newcastle Infirmary. Anna was very ill and the medications, while allowing her to sleep, had wreaked havoc with her physical health. My beautiful daughter had been reduced to a trembling wreck with a swollen tongue, unable to speak properly, hands with tremors, drooling, and eyes that looked at me with fear and distrust. What had they done? How had we arrived at such a place? How could I help her now?

The first couple of days Anna remained in a private room with putrid gray-green walls, a single bed and a night stand. The entire unit was rancid with the smell of stale smoke and institutional food. It was stark and depressing, not at all an atmosphere for healing the mind. The doctors reduced Anna's medication and her speech returned to normal, but she continued to have tremors and she remained very jittery. She was allowed to leave her room and go to smoke with the other patients, and this gave her some control over her confinement.

She remained fairly calm until Colin came to visit and then she became easily agitated. Colin started going with her to the bathroom and we all suspected that he was bringing her drugs. I begged the staff to stop him and run a drug tox screen, something that was supposed to be done on her arrival on the unit. I repeatedly asked about the original results as I thought this might give me some leeway with the doctors when they discovered that she had indeed been taking drugs; however, Colin had once again worked his magic with the receiv-

ing nurse and the original urine sample went missing. I had nothing to prove that Anna had been receiving drugs. Her diagnosis might have been different if I had been allowed to discuss any of these things with the doctors. I was told in no uncertain terms that I no longer had any say in Anna's care as Colin was now her guardian and he would be making all the decisions.

At the same time I had to find a place to stay in Newcastle as I couldn't afford a hotel. Anna's boss at Hadrian's Lodge offered me a room in his home, which was very kind of him considering all the problems he was having at the moment. My new lodgings were at great distance from the hospital and Colin had forbade me access to Anna's car, so I had a two-hour journey back and forth between the hospital and my room. I had never felt so alone and helpless in all my life. Evil has a way of making one wonder what life is really all about.

After the first few days of Anna's confinement she was moved from her private room to a ward with several other women. She was devastated as was I. I had hoped she would stay in a private room, but apparently that room was just for newcomers who were being calmed down. Long-term patients stayed in huge wards. How could this chaos favor healing? I came, I went, I visited with other patients, some who were very observant. One in particular, a young man of East Indian heritage, called me Mother and told me I had kind eyes. He also said that they were different from that man who came to visit Anna. "He has evil eyes."

Anna had some other visitors as well. Derek came one day and I don't think I have ever seen a young man more devastated than when he saw Anna. Colin, in the interim, went to London to attempt to borrow money from Anna's father. Anna wanted her father to come and visit but he did not. Perhaps he was afraid of the whole scene. Our family friend John also came to see Anna. He always thought of Anna as one of his own and had shown her much kindness over the years we had lived in England. He was very angry with the whole idea of her being ill, the drugs and Colin. If Colin had been there at the time he would have faced the wrath he so deserved.

As the days went on Anna was given more privileges and we were allowed to leave the hospital grounds and go to the corner store to buy cigarettes. I must admit I was very afraid on our first trip to the store. I did not know what Anna would do as she continued to be very angry, blaming me for her confinement. The next few days went well but all too soon it came time for me to return home to the States.

Leaving Anna in that terrible place was the worst day of my life, and knowing that Colin was now her guardian made me lose all hope for her recovery. I feared that I might never see her again. I can only say that the evil we encountered during this time period made me a believer that malevolence really exists and that, even while writing this story, he lurks at the edges of my mind and I still encounter him in nightmares.

Life on the Ward

Wellness does not result from focusing on illness. To be well one must take on a set of beliefs that encourage and promote wellness. If you believe it, it will be so. The doctors, the interns and the nurses all poked and prodded at my mind asking questions, many over and over again. They filled me with drugs to enable easier communication. They watched and debated what was wrong with me. Schizophrenia, perhaps, or bipolar disorder? The symptoms of the two illnesses mimic each other: ideas of grandeur, conversations with people/entities that aren't present, delusions, and incomprehensible thoughts that race through one's mind at breakneck speed. It took them two weeks to reach a diagnosis. My new label was bipolar disorder. Now came the treatment regime.

Locking patients in a psychiatric hospital is supposed to encourage and enable the completion of normal daily activities on a consistent basis. Once one begins to master this enforced normality, and is able to continue the regime for several days in a row, they begin to consider one ready for release. One is deemed well enough to be thrown back into the world, rehabilitated to societal standards; however, the underlying problems remain. Medication can sedate a patient into compliance with daily norms, but drugs mask symptoms and disguise whether or not one is truly well.

People with bipolar disorder are told repeatedly that they will have to spend their life on medication to control the episodes of mania and depression. I, too, was condemned to a life of medication, which doesn't seem so bad if one can ignore the side effects. The medications took away my ability to laugh wholeheartedly, cry when I was sad. They damaged my liver, caused acne, body tremors, completely destroyed my sexual desire and general joy of life. When you begin to add it up, these things take away the very reasons that living is wonderful. I went from a manic high, which was by far the greatest emotionally intense experience of my life, to being drugged into a jabbering, drooling idiot. The daily regimen of drugs was designed to stabilize my moods and prevent mania. In other words, to completely prevent my ever enjoying life again.

To hasten my departure from the hospital, I played the game. I learned to make my bed, get dressed in the morning, eat all my meals, and smoke myself silly because I knew this is what I had to do to get out. (Smoking is never discouraged as cessation may encourage the exchange of one addiction for another.) I swaggered around, full of myself and acted nastily toward other patients. I believed that I had just had a little "episode" and needed to get on with my life. In actuality, I was still in a very fragile frame of mind.

Visitors came intermittently. I could see their fear immediately upon their arrival. While on medication I was docile but had a frightening appearance. Medication made my tongue swell and I drooled. When I was not on medication I was pissed off at the world and out of control. Visitors to the ward witnessed me, and my wardmates in every degree of psychosis and "treatment." Compared to some of the patients my visitors could observe, I was not so unstable. Within a mental hospital ward, there is no separation of cases. It is also difficult to tell whether a patient's behavior is a result of their illness or their medication. My visitors probably realized that there was little separation between us and them.

The only person who visited regularly was Colin. I am still not sure why he hung in there with me for so long. I talked to other people on the phone, because they would not come to visit. I had one conversation with my stepmother, Nancy, during which I asked her if she had ever walked the thin line between sanity and insanity. "Yes," she replied. "Then it could just have easily been you in here," I told her.

During my third week I was given a day pass as a trial run to see how I'd do off hospital grounds. Colin picked me up and we took our dog Romey to the park. It was disorienting to be in the outside world. I'm not sure I could have managed my day out without an escort. I had been sequestered from current news and from the pandemonium of life beyond the ward walls. The hospital, even with its unstable patients, was a very controlled environment. Conversations, meals and visitors all came at predicable times. Inside, I focused solely on functions needed for release. Once outside for a day, the reality of my situation set in: I had once again lost everything, my job, my home, my purpose. I was, once more, going to have to start over from scratch.

In order to leave, I had to face three doctors, two interns and a nurse, and present a "plan" for my life after my release, with "evidence of a support network." I had little support and certainly no network, having alienated most all of my friends and relatives. I made one up.

Colin begged my dad to come up to Newcastle, and together the three faced the panel. The interview began with lots of questions. How are you feeling today? How are the meds working for you? Who will help you get adjusted when you are released? Do you know why you were hospitalized? Do you understand the importance of controlling the manic outbursts? I was interrogated for an hour and then asked to leave while Colin and my father were drilled. All went well and I received a day pass, which allowed me to go out, supervised, during the days but I had to return by 6 P.M. and spend the nights in the hospital. I had hoped for more but it was a step in my intended direction. I wondered how they decided to release me on only a day pass. To me, I seemed to be acting as a normal member of society.

After a week of day passes I was released for good. I went out into the world with a brand new label. The thoughts running through my mind were: I am bipolar and I now carry the stigma that goes along with being labeled mentally ill.

Depression Comes Again
Newcastle, London, New York, and London
(August 1997 to November 1998)

"It is as if my life were magically run by two electric currents: joyous and positive and despairing negative; whichever is running at the moment dominates my life, floods it. I am now flooded with despair, almost hysteria, as if I were smothering."

–Sylvia Plath

Getting out, rather than getting well, had been my primary goal for the last twenty-eight days. I would have gladly accepted any plan to get out of the hospital, so I never thought about what would happen when I was finally released. The prescribed psychiatric drugs controlled my manic episodes but did nothing about encroaching depression. My mood had swung from the highest high back down to the lowest low. Leaving the hospital literally shocked my system back into depression.

I was supposed to go to group therapy every week to ease my transition back to the real world. Attending group therapy was the worst thing imaginable. Within my group were many severely mentally ill people. They could no better support me back to wellness than I could them because the sessions were focused totally on our illnesses and how to cope with being mentally ill. Some group members were already off the deep end, and I was barely clinging to the diving board. I stopped taking the medication and going to the doctor. I gave up group, and went back to lying in bed all day, barely eating or talking. I walked little and mainly did nothing at all. Colin and I were living in a friend's apartment in an isolated town by the sea. Eventually even Colin could not take care of me and we had no place to go.

We moved to London with my dad and his family for a while. There were eight people living in a fifteen-hundred-square-foot house: Colin and me, my father and stepmother, three children, a nanny, and a constant stream of visitors. The activity put me on constant edge. I had no privacy and there was no calm. I would not stay on the medications because they made me feel so bad. It became my stepmother's mission to get me back on meds. We'd go to the doctor and get a new brand of antidepressant and I would take them for a few days. The drugs made me feel drunk and created within me anxiety and restlessness. My head would feel like it was being squeezed, I'd get dizzy and want to throw up, and would stop taking the drugs. In my depression, I wanted to be alone and there was no place to go. I felt worse on the medication than off. I could not communicate this effectively to my family. Eventually they threw me out.

I moved to New York and stayed with my brother and his wife, Yvette, for five months. They had a tiny apartment in which my sister-in-law's schizophrenic mother also lived. She had experienced age regression back to the point at which she had been pregnant with Yvette and her twin sister. She was quite harmless but exhibited many classic signs of her disease such as delusions and frequent rages. I was afraid I'd become her.

For days at a time I lay in front of the TV watching reruns. I could not have gotten a job, even if I had wanted to, since I did not have the proper visa, social security card or driver's license. I spent a lot of time in New York thinking about how wonderful mania had been and how unfortunate it was that the world didn't appreciate it. My nephew was born in March and I had been a burden to my brother and his wife for long enough. I believed that they didn't need me around while they bonded with their new arrival. I went back to London.

The Ultimate Betrayal

By the time I returned Colin had commandeered an apartment for us. Our landlord's name was Wilson. The apartment was definitely a work in progress. We called it "the cave." In the apartment's total five-hundred square feet there were no windows, no finished walls, and a leaky ceiling. It rains a lot in London, and when the rain stopped outside it continued to drip inside for days. At least it was our own space and I was surrounded by my furniture and personal effects. We cut a hole in the brick wall to make a window but did not have enough money to finish it so we covered it with a board. After another four months of sleeping and sitting around I tried working again. There had to have been a higher power helping me out as I do not know how I functioned.

Then the Ultimate Betrayal occurred: Colin left me for my stepmother. It was my own personal *Jerry Springer* episode unfolding right in front of me. I learned about this development from my dad, who had been kicked to the curb to make room for Colin. My rage finally shifted from my mother to Colin and Nancy. I now had the Ultimate Betrayal on which to focus.

It was shocking and difficult to comprehend. How could this be? Two people from my inner circle engaged in an affair? How long had it been going on? How on earth were they explaining their actions to the three young children still living in the house? "Oh by the way, your mentally ill half-sister's fiancé is now mommy's new boyfriend, and he's going to live with us! Oh, yes, and your dad and I are getting a divorce. Daddy will be moving out to make room for Colin!" My mind raced with rage and horror to imagine how this conversation was playing out on the home front. I wondered to myself how the F*#k

I was ever going to get well with all this intense stress and drama playing out around me. What the hell kind of life was this?

For the first time in my life I experienced deep hate and resentment. I spent hours mulling over ways that I could destroy their lives. Rage and poison coursed through my veins. I cried, shouted, and contemplated how I could hurt them both. I wished Colin and Nancy dead. I wished I knew a hit man to take them down. My thoughts scared me. I had never wished harm upon anyone, other than myself, before. I wasn't sure where this new set of thoughts might lead. Would I, could I, act on this? I didn't know if, since I'd already lost my mind, I could lose my moral compass as well. My anguish was all consuming. The hatred was its own kind of madness, different than mania or depression, yet equally as devastating.

The situation seemed to bond my father and me further until one day I arrived home from work to find my father's Last Words. He left a suicide note and then disappeared off the face of the earth. I found him days later in a pub south of London. He had taken sleeping pills with a vodka chaser. Not enough to kill himself but enough to cause wild hallucinations. He wandered over the moors of England, convinced that he had lost his children. He persuaded an entire village of people to help find them. A taxi driver took him around for days. By the time I came across him I knew that I had to figure out how to get us both away from the pub. No matter where my father went he always ended up owing somebody money. Neither of us had any. Somehow we managed to leave with a promise to repay what he owed to people for helping him "find his children."

We were two peas in a pod now, a pair of wayward souls. We didn't talk much about my demons or his, though they were much the same. He had dealt with his life by self-medicating with alcohol. I was following his lead though with marijuana. Smoking pot had become much more than recreational for me. I would smoke a joint a day, at least, just to get through. It was the only thing that numbed my pain.

Through work I met new friends and we planned a trip to Amsterdam. My favorite place! I could drink coffee, smoke pot and write in my journal all day long. We went for a long weekend during which I began to experience intervals of drug-induced mania. I have since learned that marijuana is one of the worst drugs a person with bipolar disorder can use.

Before my trip, my landlord, his son and I decided that the son would become my roommate when Colin moved out. When I returned from Amsterdam my apartment and furniture had been taken over by the landlord's son, who had decided that he wanted the space for himself. He changed the locks and I was homeless. I crawled in through the non-window to retrieve clothes. With no money and no car I had no way to repossess my furniture. I had to leave behind antiques from my mom, full sets of china and crystal, and all my personal papers and photographs.

My friend Richard, who was just as emotionally disturbed as I, was able to offer me a place to stay. I was out of the cold but certainly not out of the woods. My father, also without a place to stay, moved in with us. Richard's fiancée had recently left him and stripped the house clean. We lived in its empty shell. My dad cooked and cleaned for us. I continued to work; I guess it was an outlet from all the drama. Even with my job I was not making enough money to survive in London and went hungry on many days. I believe now that my dad took money from me to settle his debts. At the time I did not want to face that my dad was essentially stealing from me. After a few months I decided it was time to leave. Within five days I packed what I could carry, used the airline flight passes I had been given by a friend, and flew to the States.

Settling in America
(November 1998 to February 1999)

I felt better the moment I boarded the airplane. As it lifted into sunny skies so did my mood. I brought with me only clothes and three hundred dollars cash, all I had left to my name. I was positively giddy, just happy to be starting over—again! Before continuing to San Antonio I spent some time in New York, during which I managed to ride the waves of encroaching mania into some new and interesting situations.

The moment I got off the plane I went directly to a local bar and I met a guy. I moved in with him two days later. He lived with his sister and they kept a kosher household, a subject with which I had no experience. With numerous rules about food preparation, handling and storage, I made constant mistakes. Meat and dairy cannot touch each other in a kosher house, nor can utensils for either food category. Shaman and his sister both spoke Arabic and had frequent "offline" conversations about my numerous mistakes. In their house, I was the shiksa, or the ill-respected non-Jewish woman. Despite our differences Shaman and I had a dramatic and tumultuous, if short-lived, relationship.

Shortly after my arrival in his house, he took me to Atlantic City with his high-rolling buddies. I had never been to Vegas or Atlantic City, or, for that matter, any gambling-centric town, and the glitz and lights were all I saw. I felt like a princess, staying in luxury suites for free, enjoying the fabulous views and eating constantly. Atlantic City was a magical wonderland to me. I never saw the dingy side. I had never gambled before, and quickly learned how to play Caribbean Stud. I arrived in Atlantic City with one hundred and fifty dollars in my pocket—my entire net worth. I could not cash just fifty dollars so I had to cash in my last hundred dollars for chips. I played and played and lost every hand. On the last hand I had four aces—a lucky break—and won five hundred dollars. This only served to feed my already rampant ego. For three days I did not sleep. I spent every moment at the spa, the tables or the restaurant. I literally bounced off the walls, spinning like a top. By the time we got back to New York I was irritable and irrational.

Then came Thanksgiving. My hosts expressed an interest in a traditional Thanksgiving dinner—which I learned is nearly impossible to prepare in a kosher house. First, I had to locate a kosher turkey. Then I had to try to prepare stuffing for a turkey without using butter, because meat and dairy cannot touch each other. I could not serve dairy with dessert. And the list went on. My hosts were of little help, growing crabbier by the minute.

Within a few weeks, my mood swinging like a pendulum, and my behavior more erratic than ever, I was asked to leave. I had no money and was traveling on "buddy passes" from airlines. Because of the holidays, I needed a place to stay for a few weeks until an available day opened up for me to fly to Texas on my pass. I stayed with my sister-in-law's brother on Long Island for a few weeks. During this period my father came through for me as he never had before. I called and asked him for food money and he wired it. I would have asked nobody else but him. Luckily he was able and willing to help. Shortly before Christmas I flew to San Antonio to live with my mom. I continued to be "up" one minute and "down" the next, crying and laughing hysterically within a span of minutes. I later learned that this is called "rapid cycling."

Home in San Antonio, Texas

San Antonio was my original destination upon leaving the U.K. As such it was supposed to provide my fresh start but the holidays interfered with a calm settling-in period. I'd escaped the dire circumstances of my living conditions in London, survived numerous escapades in New York, and arrived home. I should have felt safe and felt better. I did not.

My brother, his wife and their son moved in with my mom, as well. Their house was not yet ready, so we were all again under one roof. I think Yvette was suffering from postpartum depression and in my fragile disposition I did not have the ability to deal with other people's suffering. I was empathetic and could feel their pain as if it were my own. (Throughout all of my manic and depressed episodes, my problem with boundaries caused much trouble in my life. I was unable to deal with my own emotions and sucked up those of other people like a sponge.) Being around others was difficult. The one bright light that shined through my sadness was my nephew. He has such a beautiful soul. He was not quite a year old at the time and walked around the world full of wonder, genuinely happy. His spirits lifted mine. We played every day and I felt peaceful when we were together.

I found a job as a waitress at a European restaurant that I could walk to from the house. I worked a split shift. The tips were good and the work was okay. I had been a waitress before so it was easy for me. While working double shifts at the restaurant I also fought an infection caused by an impacted wisdom tooth. I had no health insurance to get my tooth fixed. I was in constant pain and rarely slept. The combination of sleep deprivation, pain killers and antibiotics threw me out of kilter into yet another full-blown manic episode. It was Christmastime and the house was full of family. It was a nice distraction; however, because of my mania, I experienced everything with ten times the sensitivity. Holidays are stressful enough when everyone is sane and grounded. I experienced exaggerated emotional responses to everything. It was clear to my family, if not to me, that I was hanging by a few threads of reason.

Just before New Year's I went to get my driver's license. There I met Gavin, a nice gentleman, a day-trader from San Francisco who was visiting his folks for the holidays. We hung around together while he was in town. His attention was a huge boost to me. Attractive and bright, he lit up my life for the few weeks I spent with him. Again, my lack of boundaries and self-esteem led me to attach too many emotions to my short time with Gavin. He invited me out to San Francisco, all expenses paid. What luck! I could not have refused such a fantastic opportunity to see San Francisco and spend time with my new friend. Throughout all of my terrifying experiences, I still managed incredible runs of luck. Had I fallen into a lake, I would have come out with fish in my pocket.

The Homecoming

Anna had finally decided to come to San Antonio. She was once again crying on the phone, hungry and alone. London had become an unbearable and terrifying experience. Anna had finally realized that even with full-time employment and a roommate, London was never going to be affordable. I was overjoyed, relieved and somewhat apprehensive. Would she really come?

Anna arrived in San Antonio several weeks later after a stay in New York, which had set her back yet again. Anna met and moved in with a man and his sister. Again money, mind games and her continuing illness led to another episode of mania followed by a descent into depression that would become suicidal.

After a couple of weeks in San Antonio recuperating from her New York experiences, Anna found a job at a local restaurant within walking distance of home and worked several shifts a week. Anna also kept busy securing a copy of her birth certificate, driver's license and green card, as all of those papers had gone missing during her illness in England. During one of her trips to the driver's license bureau she met Gavin from San Francisco. They began dating and he and his mother spent New Year's with us in San Antonio. A few days later Gavin returned to San Francisco, but not before inviting Anna out to visit him. Anna had readily accepted and, with misgivings, I watched her planning a trip that she didn't have the stamina or health to make. I knew I should not have let her go; however, I felt that I had no other choice. Unfortunately at the same time she came down with a very painful impacted wisdom tooth and was prescribed antibiotics and pain killers.

Crazy in San Francisco
(January 1999)

On the day I was to leave for San Francisco I had a difficult time packing my suitcase. I could not hold my thoughts together very well. My ego inflated and deflated like a balloon. Because of my heightened awareness and sensitivity, I flew into rages easily and unpredictably and had quit my job the night before when the restaurant owner pushed my buttons. I was bound and determined to get on the plane and get out of San Antonio so I did what I could to get it together. My brother drove me to the airport and I made my flight.

I had not been sleeping well and the lack of rest made it hard think and reason. Though I knew little about how to control my moods, thoughts and feelings, I knew that sleep helped me stay calmer and more even tempered, even in the midst of my madness. I decided to sleep on the flight, but it was too late, the balance had tipped too far toward mania. My three hours of sleep on the plane were not enough to bring me back to reality. I arrived in San Francisco paranoid and shaking. To Gavin I appeared to be frenetic and giddy. I was actually hallucinating. I know we made a couple of stops between the airport and his home but my memories of that experience remain a blur.

Gavin's apartment was wonderful. It sat high up on a hill and overlooked the Bay. I forgot about sleeping, concentrating or doing any normal activity. Instead I constantly oscillated between agitation, feeling trapped and feeling overwhelmed with happiness and lightheaded giddiness.

On the second day of my long weekend, I was supposed to drive to Gavin's office in his car to have lunch with him. I locked myself out of the apartment, and thus out of car keys, so I had to walk to meet him. I was extremely late and he was upset. That was the last bit of normality during my visit. I took a walk down to Fisherman's Wharf while Gavin was at work. I walked along the pier and stopped for a drink. I spent the afternoon imagining being in San Francisco with everyone I know. I visited with Gavin's neighbor who lived in the apartment above. We smoked pot and talked for hours. I drank some root beer, which made me think of my grandfather and his gas station. He would always pop the cap on a bottle of root beer or grape soda when we'd drop by to visit him. I sat with Gavin's neighbor, talking to my grandfather. Each sip brought me closer to his memory, deeper into conversation with him. With each sip I slipped further from reality.

That evening Gavin and I went to a tiny neighborhood restaurant with some of his friends. I could not sit still, and paced and stalked the floor of the restaurant. I did not eat three bites of dinner. Gavin and his friends did the best they could to deal with me. I was to fly home the next day, a sure relief for them. We still had to make it through the long night.

Gavin called my mother and they talked about my baffling behavior. She told him everything that she could about keeping watch over me and not leaving me alone. I was not sleeping, so Gavin and his friends could not either. They took shifts watching me so I would not escape from the apartment. I felt I was their prisoner. They just wanted to put me on a plane. In the morning, though I was scheduled for a late-night flight, Gavin took me to the airport, dropped me at the door and bid me farewell.

So much for keeping watch. By that time I convinced myself that all bad things would come if I returned to San Antonio. I decided not to get on the flight. My brother and his wife were fighting a lot when I left. My mother would no doubt have grand plans for my treatment. I looked up at the departure information and saw a flight to London Heathrow. I was relived; I could go home to England. I had no money for a plane ticket but that did not stop me from dreaming of going somewhere else. I did not go to England nor did I leave

San Francisco. I had no plan, but in my hypermania I believed that I was the one with all the answers and everything would work itself out eventually.

I spent a few hours sitting in the airport, furiously writing my thoughts. I got a few strange looks from some airport workers, who were more concerned than anything. Feeling sorry for me, they got me a cup of coffee and a place to sit in the employee lounge. I decided to take a cab back to the city. I cannot remember where I got out or how I paid for the taxi. Apparently I found my way back to Gavin's apartment and then escaped again before I could be sent back to San Antonio. I remember nothing of that part of my story, which my mother recounts in the following chapter.

In my mania I believed I was connected to all people and could see their innermost thoughts and assumed, therefore, they could see mine. I traveled from one all-night diner to the next, drinking coffee, writing and waiting for Gavin to come meet me again. He would know, through my cosmic connection, where I was and come rescue me. Of course, at the time, not a soul in the world knew where I was but I believed everyone did.

I spent some time in doorways and walking up and down the hilly streets of San Francisco. I spoke with fellow homeless people along my travels, loving each and every one of them. I stayed out all night. I went to one of the squares where the birds loved me. I communicated with them. When I said "fly," they flew. If I said "rest," they landed all around me.

While sitting near Golden Gate Bridge, I decided to have a family conference. San Francisco was one place where my mom, my dad and I had all been. For my conflict-resolution session I decided to get coffee for each of us. Mom liked lattes, my dad took his black with sugar, and I drank cappuccinos. We were all going to sit by the water and talk—telepathically. I got everyone's coffee just the way they liked it but something happened in the coffee shop to agitate me. I started throwing cups around and was asked to leave. A police officer approached me and told me that if I did not move on he would arrest me. San Francisco is full of eccentric people; so to be noticed by the police and surrounding people I must have been acting unusually erratically. After I talked to him, I went back into the coffee shop, bent on getting coffee for my family reunion. The next thing I knew I was handcuffed and put in the back of a police car. The police officer sighed as deep a sigh as I have ever heard and drove me away. He was upset by my appearance, sorry that he had to arrest me and doubtful that anything could be done to help. I had wandered aimlessly for forty-eight hours.

He took me to a hospital and I was admitted to the mental health ward. My paperwork read: Indigent, next of kin unknown, homeless runaway. At the time, I was twenty-seven years old, but I looked like a minor. It is good that I really was indigent as listed, or I would have had a huge hospital bill from my next fourteen days in the psych ward.

Hospitalization Number Two

During my two days on the streets of San Francisco I visited many restaurants and wrote tons of post cards that I never mailed. I'm not sure who I was writing them to. I was almost grateful for being arrested so I could get some sleep. I was sure that my mother would be called and be informed that I was safe, that I would get a good night's sleep and fly to San Antonio the next day. For a while, though admitted for mental-health reasons, I was allowed to roam free throughout the hospital ward.

Because this was my second manic episode, the medical professionals were convinced I needed medication for life to control the outbursts. I was to have regular visits to the doctor for blood work to make sure the medication was within therapeutic levels. I refused to take the same medications they had offered me before. Only the threat of electroshock therapy made me stay on my medicine. During my stay on the psychiatric ward I went to therapy sessions and I kept a detailed notebook. I was, again, clearly fixated on trying to get out. Manic depression had become my identity.

Several days after my arrival I called my mom, indignant that she knew where I was and had not bothered to call me. (The only way my mom knew of my location was from speaking with Gavin. I thought she would have known where I was because, after all, I was cosmically connected to everyone and everything.) Gavin came to call. I could see the terror on his face as we sat amongst the drooling, unsocial, outrageous characters that populated the visiting tables of the mental hospital. He visited only once.

As in the hospital in Newcastle, patients daily caused scenes. There were scheduled electroshock therapy sessions for some, medicines for others, and the same definition of "well": taking care of daily hygiene, eating regularly, taking medicine, and apparent emotional stability.

The doctors decided not to release me at the end of the fourteen days. Someone would have to come and get me and take responsibility for my care. It was deeply embarrassing that I was a grown woman but needed a caretaker in order to be released. My mom flew out, picked me up and took me back to San Antonio.

A Missing-person Report

Anna was heading for mania again as she worked extra shifts and packed for her trip to San Francisco. I continued to worry that this was not a good idea. I tried to speak with her about this trip, but she was so determined that there was nothing I could do to stop her. I went to meet Anna at the airport on the day of her expected arrival, and to my horror she did not show up. Frantic, I contacted the airlines and they told me that no Anna Malden had boarded their flight from San Francisco to San Antonio. I started to make calls to San Francisco. Gavin he told me he had dropped her off at the airport in the early morning on the date of her departure. He had no idea where Anna was nor had Anna been honest with him from the beginning. After I explained her probable fragility of mind and how she had problems with getting on airplanes when her illness escalated he offered to help look for her. I also called the San Francisco police and explained that my daughter was ill and alone in the streets of San Francisco and begged them to do their utmost to find her. Gavin and friends of his found Anna sitting outside their apartment building and managed to get her inside. As Anna's behavior had now escalated to a full-blown manic episode, her behavior frightened Gavin and he had placed her in a vacant apartment for the night. Gavin and I were speaking on the phone hourly. When I heard he had left her alone in a friend's apartment I warned him that she would not stay there. Unfortunately my prediction came true. Anna was once again out on the street and alone with only her disordered thoughts for company.

Anna's chaotic mind led to a confrontation in a local restaurant—she was throwing cups—and they called the police. Thank goodness I had already called the police and they knew her story. They took her to the local psychiatric *hospital instead of a jail cell. Anna was in the middle of another nightmare.*

Anna was confined to the psychiatric hospital in San Francisco for two weeks, and during this time I had several conversations with a social worker. These calls mainly concerned what Anna was going to do and where she would live when she was released. His main concern was that I would come to San Francisco to ensure she would not be released into the streets. We set a date for Anna's release and I made plans to bring her home.

I went directly from the airport to the hospital and on ringing the admittance bell was confronted with a bearded man who was drooling and snarling like a rabid animal. I had to pass this apparition while ensuring that he did not get out the door. The nurses gave me a frosty reception and directed me to the smoking area. Once again Anna had tremors, lithium doing its worst. She was still talking very fast, mainly nonsense, and continually pacing. I was afraid of what she might do when we left the hospital.

We went out for dinner, but Anna had a difficult time sitting still for any length of time. We returned to our hotel but neither of us could sleep. I was terrified that if I fell asleep she would leave and start the nightmare all over again. I don't recall how we got back to the airport or the journey home.

The Great Depression, Round Three

San Antonio, Austin

(February 1999 to October 2000)

I arrived back from San Francisco off my rocker again. I crashed into a deep black hole of depression. I had such potential, sitting there in the self-discovery workshop, but over a few years, I became my diagnosis. I was my illness; I was only a manic depressive. It was so hard the first and second time and now I was in round three. I thought "I just want to die. This life is too hard for me, I'm overwhelmed with trying, there's nothing here for me."

My thoughts continued their downward spiral, and I climbed into bed and wished the world away. At that point I could no longer deny what had happened. I could not write off each situation as a fluke or nervous breakdown caused by stress. I had to own my identity. I was a mentally ill person. I suffered from a bipolar disorder. I was sick. Not only that, I was worthless, useless and undeserving of a good life.

I was scared and had no idea how to rebuild my life. I thought of the mentally unstable people I had met in my life and how I had felt about them, how I didn't want to have to look at them or deal with them. I felt ashamed for how I had thought about these people and knew my fate was similar to theirs. People would always look at me differently, always respond with sympathy or fear that my problems would rub off on them.

I was angry and frustrated that medications did not work. Everyone was concerned about controlling my attacks of mania, not at all worried about my depression. Mania is not a socially acceptable behavior, so it is taken care of quickly. Depression is a reserved and inward-facing plight with little outward impact, so it's not as pressing to the world at large. A depressed person suffers in silence.

In a last-ditch attempt to get me back on my feet mom took me to one more psychiatrist. At last, after several years, someone prescribed a combination of drugs that actually worked. At first the drugs knocked me out and I slept most of the day for a week. When I finally got up, it didn't feel so bad. My mind no longer raced. The knot in my stomach was gone. The pain in my heart had subsided and I felt like a normal person, smiling a little, enjoying the taste of food and taking in sensory data.

This was a remarkable feeling considering the alternative. I had been on the brink of taking my own life—lacking only the gumption and the energy to do it. The medicines were enough to help me get a grip and begin rebuilding a life. I decided that I would never accomplish anything spectacular with my life and began to give myself over to the identity of sickness. In so doing, I began to bask in the safety of no responsibility and low expectations. For the first time in my life I put no pressure on myself to be anything but well. I lowered my stress by lowering my expectations, and began to recover.

I couldn't trust myself, so I surely didn't want others to trust or depend on me. At the same time I was desperate for my independence and to get away from all the talk of sickness. I wanted a fresh start. I responded to a job advertisement for trainer at a bank in Austin, Texas. They called me for an interview. It took all the courage I could muster to drive myself to the appointment. It was an all day multiperson interview process and it was hard for me. It had been a long time since I had made small talk, tried to be charming and sold myself.

By the grace of God I made it through the day and soon was offered the job. It was amazing. They didn't know I was ill; I had a chance at a fresh start but wondered if I was strong enough to handle the responsibility. Taking the job would mean moving to a new city where I didn't know anyone and starting over again, all by myself. I was terrified but I accepted the offer. Afterwards I got really panicky. I called back and told them I couldn't take the job. I made up some story about family problems back in the U.K. that I had to take care of. After the call, I couldn't believe what I had done: I'd just thrown out the window my ticket back to life.

I forced myself to call again and let them know that I could start but it would be a later date and they agreed to it. I was in disbelief. I had accepted the offer, rejected the offer and then got another offer! It really made me wonder who was driving the bus in my life. It seemed that the control and lack thereof from the last few years was simply an illusion. It seemed that the best way to enjoy this life was to jump on and enjoy the ride. The train is already moving and we are merely passengers.

The Way Back

Back home Anna was jittery with intermittent bouts of relative calm and had days of depression that left her almost catatonic. She slept much of the time. Her waking hours were filled with weeping or staring into space. I knew she was on the verge of suicide and we were seeking help every way we could. Unlike England, where National Health Care assisted in Anna's recovery, in the United States Anna had no health insurance. We were forced to seek free services. At one appointment Anna sat for several hours and was turned away because the doctor was too busy to see her. Anna was suicidal and the doctor was too busy to give assistance. Her lack of insurance made her invisible to everyone but me. I was desperate. One of the nurses at work recommended a psychiatrist of good reputation who had helped a member of her family.

I contacted Dr. Kholi and explained Anna's condition and our plight with no insurance. Dr. Kholi, a psychiatrist from India, said she would see Anna for fifty dollars a visit, and thus began our relationship with a true Good Samaritan. Dr. Kholi examined Anna and then spoke to me in no uncertain terms regarding what had to be done. The good doctor ordered three prescription drugs. She told me that Anna was at high risk for suicide and that she could not be left alone for any reason. This assessment of Anna's mental status was not a surprise, but hearing it from a psychiatric professional frightened me beyond measure. I was at risk of losing my daughter, my precious child. I was not going to let that happen!

If anyone doubts that mental illness is exacerbated by a disorder of brain chemicals, this was illustrated in spades when, after a week of Dr. Kholi's prescriptions Anna got up and about and began to take part in life again. After seeing scores of doctors over several years and being given various drug combinations, this one was working. She was not yet well but she was so much better that I rejoiced for the miracle that was unfolding.

Moving to Austin

I was low on confidence and unsure of myself but I managed to pack my life and drive myself to Austin to start again. I arrived in Austin with corporate accommodations for the first month so I had time to find a place to live. I started work and daily I battled fear, uncertainty and anxiety. My confidence levels were low. The act of keeping myself together was exhausting. I simply hoped the armor did not crack in public. At the end of each day I went home overwhelmed and crying. The best time of day was bedtime: no more expectations; I could close my eyes and make the world disappear for a few hours. I still thought maybe I would not wake up. I thought that would be great.

I woke each morning exhausted, battling to get out bed and make it to the office on time. I was typically running five to fifteen minutes late every day. Even though I was salaried, the people that I trained punch a clock and got fired for being one or two minutes late. I was supposed to be setting the example. Being late was not acceptable.

I continued to struggle like this for a few months. I kept starting and stopping the medications. Although the drugs helped me cope they did come with a heavy price. The side effects included headaches, nausea, lack of energy and feelings of disconnection from everything and everyone. Eventually I forced myself to learn how to live with my condition and think myself well.

Anna in Austin

Once again Anna was going away. She had a job in Austin. She would be alone there and I was not sure she was strong enough to manage on her own. I visited as often as I could and always came away knowing that she was struggling while putting on a brave face. Anna continued to forge ahead and I watched with great pride as she started to make new friends and manage a career while coping with as many bad days as good.

My Journey to Wellness

– PART II –

"Do not believe what you have heard. Do not believe in tradition because it was handed down by many generations. Do not believe in anything that has been spoken of many times. Do not believe because the written statement comes from some old sage. Do not believe in authority or teachers or elders. But after careful observation and analysis, when it agrees with reason and it will benefit one and all, then accept it and live by it."

–Buddha

The road to wellness holds a great conundrum: It is exceedingly difficult to get well when one doesn't feel well. I was reminded of this recently when I came down with a severe cold. For the first couple of days my patience was high and I spent each day caring for myself and just being still to allow my body to repair itself. By day three my patience was waning and I questioned why I got sick and why I wasn't getting well. Fully perplexed by my symptoms, I was grouchy, frustrated and beginning to feel depressed. I oscillated between thoughts of being grateful that I have my health (most of the time) and thoughts of how life is not worth much without it. As I contemplated the pointlessness of all activities I was amazed at how quickly my slide into dark thought patterns came on. This seven-day bout of a wintertime cold reminded me how thin the veil between meaning and pointlessness is. Bipolar episodes of mania and depression are nothing more than extremes of the highs and lows that life brings. Will today be filled with joy, peace, love and the beauty of life or will it be filled with fear, hatred and disgust for this life experience? Isn't this conflict the very thing that vexes us humans most?

I contemplated for some time how I might handle the tricky nature of writing this section. It was difficult because I am aware that the journey for each of us is unique and that the gift I give to you is in my personal discovery of truth, love and freedom. In the following section, you will go with me as I walk my path to recovery. My journey through the peaks and valleys will look different than yours because there are so many paths. Many masters have gone before us and offer us signposts. "This way" their messages echo. Perhaps you will find my story another signpost to help you along your way.

I wanted to prepare an offering that would meet each individual where he or she is and provide enough choices so that each reader could find their own starting place: a place wherein you can connect to your own life-fulfilling story rather than a life of suffering. Here I offer a way for each of you to *Meet Yourself in the Middle* between the emotional highs and lows from your birth through death on Planet Earth. Welcome to the opportunity to truly know who you are and experience your life as it was intended. Be free my friend, free to love, free to create, and free to be just as you are.

I am certain that each of us can achieve peace, love and freedom in this life. What you'll find here is an offering of ideas, resources and maps that can help you on the journey. Take what works, leave what doesn't and know that you are perfect exactly as you are. My greatest wish for you is that you develop the art of conscious choice in all decisions related to your life. You decide…You discover…You create your life!

My Journey to Wellness Begins

After the San Francisco debacle I could no longer chalk up my experiences to bad luck, being in the wrong place at the wrong time or a nervous breakdown with bouts of depression. I had reached the time when I could no longer deny the problem. I had to accept that I was mentally ill, and deal with it.

The Road Not Taken
Two roads diverged in a yellow wood,
And sorry I could not travel both
And be one traveler, long I stood
And looked down one as far as I could
To where it bent in the undergrowth;

Then took the other, as just as fair,
And having perhaps the better claim,
Because it was grassy and wanted wear;
Though as for that the passing there
Had worn them really about the same,

And both that morning equally lay
In leaves no step had trodden black.
Oh, I kept the first for another day!
Yet knowing how way leads on to way,
I doubted if I should ever come back . . .

I shall be telling this with a sigh
Somewhere ages and ages hence:
Two roads diverged in a wood, and I—
I took the one less traveled by,
And that has made all the difference.

–Robert Frost, Mountain Interval, 1906

Most who read Robert Frost's poem interpret it as a sort of declaration of independence. Careful analysis of the poem reveals its meaning to be different than what it appears at first glance. Frost's words describe a walker making a choice, with the outcome uncertain. You can choose a conventional path or an unconventional path. The act of choosing, rather than letting someone choose for you, is the act of independence. Whether you settle on the conventional route or the controversial route is not necessarily important. As you walk it you encounter more choices. You choose again and then live with your choices. *Yet knowing how way leads on to way/I doubted if I should ever come back.* You cannot change your past but you can choose which path to walk in the future, and you keep walking and you keep choosing. Independence is not going against the crowd. Independence is choosing your own way.

Prior to San Francisco, my "normal" life included drama, betrayal and events fit only for the *Jerry Springer Show*. I had accepted my situation because I felt there was no other alternative. I believed, wholeheartedly, that I had fallen victim to a dangerous, treacherous, impassable world. I thought that I had, and would continue to have, no control, say or responsibility in any of it. My lot was my destiny and I often wondered why I had drawn the short straw. Did I have bad karma, bad parents or bad genes? Because my suffering continued, despite many different efforts to the contrary, I always assumed that I deserved what I got.

My Choice

My journey to wellness began exactly three years after my first round of clinical depression in August 1996. In August 1999 I had reached the fork in the road and made the decision that I wanted to be well. I wanted to be more than a bipolar label. I made a choice.

Recovering from mental illness is no different than recovery from addiction. Hospital intake forms lump the two together: "We the undersigned, allege, that the above-named person is, as a result of mental disorder or impairment by chronic alcoholism: (1) a danger to others, (2) a danger to himself or herself (3) gravely disabled . . ."

The process of recovery is similar as well. The twelve-step program that alcoholics and other addicts have been using for decades offers a "how to" methodology that has worked for many people. I did not participate in an official twelve-step program; however, upon reflection, my journey to wellness has been a series of steps. I am walking my own twelve-step journey.

The steps themselves provide a framework and approach to life that I make everyday.

Step One —
Making Peace with Where I Am

It was apparent that my life had become unmanageable. I decided to stop fighting the diagnosis, the medications, my internal chaos, and external factors I had blamed for my illness and its consequences. I took a deep breath and made peace with where I was right then. The most difficult part of this step was fully realizing where I was and what I would have to do to get well. At twenty-seven years old, I was unable to support myself, I lived with my mom, I had no friends, no hobbies, no money in the bank, and no idea how to begin again. I was at rock bottom. I prayed for the last time.

I only sank deeper into depression when I thought about the past. Similarly, if I mused too much about the future I got anxious wondering if I would need a caretaker for my entire life. I realized that I could not make peace with where I was if I was always rummaging around in the past. I also could not make peace with myself if I was fearful of future events. I had to stop living in the past, worrying about the future and live in the present. Making peace with me, in the present, was the first step on the road to wellness. Once I accepted my situation as it was, and said it out loud, lived it and was it, I felt a sense of peace flood my body and for the first time in three years I felt calm. If the sensation had a voice it would have whispered in my ear "Now you can get well. None of what has happened really matters. It's time; you can rebuild your life. All is well."

Step Two—
Deciding To Be Well

After three years of torment, I did not feel calm for long. Negative thoughts crept back into my head. Because my mind had been conditioned to feed me negative suggestions, it would take time and effort to break this pattern. My moment of calm gave a glimmer of hope that there was something beyond my current status. It was a small flash of light, no bigger than a pin hole, but enough to lead me to decide and affirm that I wanted to be well. I wanted to be happy, to love, to laugh, to desire, to join in, to be normal.

I have never known what normal meant at any stage of my life. I have always been something of a misfit, using my chameleon-like ability to fit in wherever I go. After years of trying to fit in I knew my own likes or dislikes about almost nothing. I have measured success by definitions of other people. For me to be normal in the context of society I would have to be healthy and without mental impairment. I wanted to achieve this so badly because I did not want to have to navigate the world with the crushing weight of a mental disability.

Deciding to be well was a bigger step for me than it first appeared to be. Sickness is a form of refuge in its own right. When I was sick no one expected much of me; I did not have to be responsible and accountable for my life. Especially with mental illness, it was easy to slink away into the corner and act crazy and get away with anything I wanted. Along with its terrible prisonlike sentence, mental illness also provided a quality of freedom from adulthood: no responsibilities, no consequences, no expectations. Society perpetuates the idea of mental illness as incapacitation, and mentally ill people are not expected to take on any responsibilities. This mindset only serves to reinforce the ill person's thoughts of uselessness and sends the message that, sick or well, the person has nothing to contribute. The most constructive way to interact with mentally ill individuals is expect of them what you would expect of anyone. This is a profoundly helpful practice. It's like throwing a rope into the darkness, tying it around their waist and pulling them up to the light. Remember who they are when they are well and hold this picture as vividly and often as you can. Offer it as sort of prayer if you will. Do no let them off the hook of responsibility. In this way you can make a huge difference.

Choosing to be well and free from mental illness also meant choosing to be responsible for my own life, happiness and direction. I would no longer view myself as subject to external factors. I chose to keep control of my own life. I had no idea how I would get well but the most important part was that I decided that I wanted it. I found that when I set my direction, the world conspired to give me what I needed, making me more peaceful and less worried about the outcome.

Step Three—
Finding Faith in a Higher Power

There is continuity to life that is invisible to the naked eye. Somehow an unseen force holds things together here on earth. You may call it God, the Universe, Allah, Higher Self, Creator, Divinity, whatever you choose. I like to use many different words to describe this higher power, and will use them interchangeably in this section.

I believe wholeheartedly in this higher power, especially after landing my first job at the beginning of the rest of my life. I interviewed and was offered a job in Austin, turned it down, called back, and was again offered the job. Up until this point the jury was out for me. I wasn't sure I believed in God, but at the same time, I couldn't believe that life was simply a matter of chance. I had spent some years thinking that if there was a god, he or she was surely pissed off, as it appeared that the god entity seemed to have left me out in the cold to fend for myself. My first Austin experience gave me the sense that something beyond my physical self is at play in my life.

Quietly, and without fanfare, I began to search for the meaning of God in my life. I read spiritual books and listened in on conversations as people talked of their beliefs. I remained open to the fact that somehow, despite all the drama and turmoil of my life, I seemed to have survived it all, for a purpose of which I was still unaware. I knew that when I was unable to care for myself, someone or something always showed up to lend a hand, which seemed to me to be more than mere coincidence. At this stage of the journey, I was content to believe that there was more at work than I could see with my eyes, hear with my ears or touch with my hands. There was a power at work and I was ready to have a relationship. By the grace of God I was in one piece and on my way to new life in Austin, Texas, where my recovery would continue.

Step Four—
Living One Day at a Time and Finding New Boundaries

I started a new job in Austin and survived my first month, barely, as you have seen. I got through the period of my new job by going through the motions: I got up, went to work, acted as though I was fine, went home and collapsed in exhaustion. Each day was a battle that I fought and won to see another day. Even though I made it through, I was still not really well.

I decided to take some classes and convinced my employer to pay for the classes and give me one day a month to attend. I continued my studies in neuro-linguistic programming (NLP). It's an applied psychology known as the art and science of excellence, teaching techniques that allowed me to access and reprogram patterns that don't serve me anymore. I was on a mission to get my head to work right, come hell or high water.

In this environment I got to share the truth of who I am. I am bipolar and I pinned my diagnosis to my chest like a badge of honor. I was angry about the diagnosis and I showed it. I was angry about the betrayal by Colin and Nancy and I wanted the world to know exactly how hard life had been for me. At the seminar I learned that my anger is part of a grieving process and could last at least eighteen months to two years. Until then I had not acknowledged that I was grieving. I had been focusing completely on my mental illness; however, in addition to my illness, recovery from damage related to family situations I'd recently been through would take some time.

The NLP community sustained me and held my hand while I cried. I learned how to grieve, how to set goals and how to find more useful ways to think and navigate the landscape of life. The classes were just what I needed and continued in three-day sets once a month for a year. Occasionally, I showed up at class and started to cry in the morning and continued to cry uncontrollably throughout the day. The teacher and the class allowed me the space to do this and supported me as I found a way to be at peace with my pain. Instead of fearing my outbursts and trying to stuff them inside, I learned that it is okay to let them out. I found more space for my emotions and thoughts and my heart began to open to others without taking in their pain and letting it affect me. I offered compassion and listened without feeling the need to run away or fix someone else's situation. I learned about boundaries and what my baggage was and wasn't. The year was a healing time for me.

Step Five—
Confessing the Truth

To right other areas in my life I also needed to assure that my work situation was working well. Being late to work almost every day was not part of the equation for success in this new work environment. I did not have the best relationship with my boss and we had several talks about my tardiness, among other things. I did not reveal to my boss the demons I was fighting. I kept working and I started to make a few friends at the smoking pavilion. I practiced socializing during my fifteen-minute breaks and lunch. Bit by bit, I became less anxious. I was not yet happy but I did not despair. I was actually numb from all of my medications but I was making it through the day. I had no real direction or purpose except to find my footing.

Though I tried to make it to work on time and do a good job, I continued to have regular run-ins with my boss. Eventually, I was written up and notified that I would be given no more leeway. I needed to be at work on time or I needed to find somewhere else to work. In order to keep my job, and continue my path to wellness, I played my trump card. I revealed that I have bipolar disorder, which gave me protection under the Americans with Disabilities Act. Because of this, they could not fire me as easily. I decided to do my part and get to work on time and called in sick less often.

Telling my boss and friends at work was a huge step for me. For once everyone knew the truth about me and I did not have to spend massive amounts of energy keeping it in. That itself let me focus my energy on getting well. I found a few friends to confide in and they stuck around despite knowing about my diagnosis. I found a roommate, so I was not so lonely when I returned home at night. Soon I met Doug, who became my husband within a year.

Step Six—
Moving Beyond the Diagnosis

Meeting Doug was like running into an old friend I had not seen in a while. He is easy to be with and really grounded. He proved to be an excellent balance for me, helping me learn what it means to be anchored. Our story of meeting is wonderful but is another book, altogether. He is the perfect partner for me. He didn't even flinch when I told him I am bipolar on our first date. He is the love of my life, my best friend and the cornerstone of my support network. Our relationship is a haven of love and friendship that I never knew was possible. Inside this safe place I was able to learn to love myself fully and, in turn, love him completely. I found that it is in our relationships that we learn to love. Our loved ones are mirrors through which we see ourselves and learn to polish away the tarnish and erase our shortcomings. I live in gratitude everyday for the honor and privilege of sharing my life with this man.

Around the time I met Doug I started to consider life beyond the medication. The psychiatric community maintains that the main problem with bipolar patients is that they feel better, stop taking their meds, and end up sick again. In reality, medication limits enjoyment of life. Anyone who has to take medication for bipolar disorder will dream of a day that they don't have to take it. Further complicating the issue, doctors prescribe medications in a try-it-and-see method. A patient-drug match is measured by the reaction of the patient. From the time of my first hospitalization I had taken no less than fifteen different types of mood stabilizers, antidepressants and anxiety medications. Most of the medications I took were not helpful. They subdued manic tendencies but plunged me into depression. Despair, suicidal thoughts and complete withdrawal from life are not something I can continually live with. When I took the medications I experienced the following side effects:

- Dry mouth
- Constipation
- Sexual dysfunction
- Blurred vision
- Dizziness
- Severe drowsiness as a daytime problem
- Increased heart rate and heart palpitations
- Low blood pressure
- Nausea
- Headaches
- Weight gain
- Stiff neck
- Chills
- Fear
- Agitation
- Anxiety
- Tremor
- Abnormal vision

The last combination of medications helped me begin to function in a somewhat normal way; however, the side effects were difficult to manage. Additionally, the medicine limited my range of emotion. I watched a sad movie and didn't cry, or saw a funny movie and did not laugh. Short-term side effects of many of the medicines are highly unpleasant. Long-term effects still have not been studied at any length. For this reason, I decided to try to find a way to live medication free.

I knew that stopping cold turkey was not a good solution, especially without a game plan. I had been down this road before and it did not work. After my third depressive episode I was sure that I could not make it through another full-blown cycle. With each round my suicidal thoughts had become more and more severe. I begin pulling together a plan to get off the meds and move beyond the diagnosis to start living my life fully.

Step Seven— Creating a Life I Want

Before I experienced my first round of clinical depression, I was convinced that cultivating the ability to think and reason on a high level was one of the most important things in my life. I judged myself and others around me based on how "smart" we were. I avidly read psychology and self-help books and attended many seminars and workshops about changing my thoughts and disciplining my mind. I now found that, even without a higher level of brain functioning, I was still here. I had not disappeared. I began to believe that our mind is much bigger than our intellect and reasoning. With this, I freed myself from the trap of becoming and rested in the reality of being.

From this vantage point I explored that depression caused by a chemical imbalance in the brain could be affected by altering my thoughts. I determined four components within my control that were affecting my brain chemistry.

1)   Nutrition: Biological processes are supported or hindered by an appropriate supply of nutrients. I could determine what to eat and drink.

2)   Sleep: The construction of the human system requires periods of rest to be fully operational. Sleep deprivation can cause hallucinations, so it stands to reason that not getting enough sleep may impact the delicate chemical balance in my brain. I could pay attention to getting enough sleep.

3)   Physiology: Mind and body are part of the same system. What affects one affects the other. I could pay attention to the needs of my body like exer-

cise, rest and freedom from stress.

4)   Thoughts: Research shows that our thinking impacts how we feel and function. Since my brain is used primarily for thinking, thoughts must have something to do with creating chemicals in my brain. I could pay attention to my thoughts; I could change my way of thinking.

Upon determining these factors, I was no longer at the whim of biology or genetics. I could take responsibility for my own health and well-being. Armed with this knowledge, I decided to find ways to stop the medication and think myself well.

To ensure my game plan was rock solid and had the best chance of success, I developed two important parts of the plan. First I made peace with myself that if my plan did not work I would go back onto the medication as needed. I would no longer consider the need for medication a failure on my part or as a lifetime necessity, but as a resource available if I need it. Second, I assembled a support network. This was the most important step in my plan to live without medication. I needed my closest friends and family to understand my plan so that they could help me if the strategy did not work as intended. I provided detailed information on what to expect and what to do if a manic episode took over my rational thoughts.

With my plan in place I began to slowly wean myself off the medication. I did not look back and it has been seven years since I popped a pill. I am vibrant, fully alive and loving life. I run my own consulting business with my husband and together we enjoy a fulfilling life with our dogs, our family and our friends. We do not yet have children but that may be in our future.

I have found ways to manage my life, listen to myself and keep my balance. Even after seven years I still pay attention to my thoughts, sleep, nutrition and the relationship between my mind and body. I know that for me to be at my best I need more sleep than the average person. I typically sleep nine to ten hours a night because I feel better when I do. My thoughts now arise from my gratitude for the wonders I experience each day and by adherence to the goals and dreams I pursue. I stay away from popular news and media. I am an empathic individual with a high sensitivity for the feelings of others. Too much exposure to mainstream media drops me back into a negative thinking pattern.

I do not diet or deprive myself of the things I love to eat. I keep a balance and stay away from over stimulating my system as much as possible. Everything I put in my body impacts its chemistry so I'm careful not to reach for over-the-counter or prescription meds too quickly. I support my body to heal itself whenever I can.

For exercise I find swimming and yoga are a good fit for me and I practice them as often as I can. I allow my body to follow its natural rhythms and cycles. Some weeks I exercise every day and others I don't go at all. I have expanded my understanding of body-mind continuum to include movement. Movement can include walking, dancing, swaying, sitting, standing and so on. All movement has an affect on my body and mind, and can shift my perspective, preventing my thinking from becoming stuck in a rut.

Step Eight— Discovering Love

After I stopped medication, I still needed to heal. After all of my experiences I had little self trust. I could not have successful relationships with others if I could not trust myself. I discovered that forgiveness is key to future happiness and it does not have to take years, as I had previously believed. I let go of my regret, resentment and rage and found a new way of seeing. I discovered tools to help me design the life I always dreamed of. I moved from being victim to being creator in my life. I became proactive rather than reactive and many new possibilities appeared. I no longer identified myself as bipolar. I am Anna, exploring, searching and seeking answers to a bigger life.

I found that true love, the kind that knows no bounds and has no conditions, is even more wonderful than the romantic notions of love I grew up with. I am still learning about true love, and through my journey my heart was cracking open. I have become more compassionate, giving and serving of myself and others than ever before. I began to discover true love by no longer judging myself and others. When I catch my mind wandering into judgmental chatter, I gently redirect it to more upbeat thoughts. I am constantly reminding myself that from my singular vantage point I can't possibly know what's really going on within another person. It serves me better to notice and accept myself and other people exactly as they are. No meaning, no analysis.

I have read somewhere that problems arise when we focus on too much on the self, and if we are in service to another we don't get so easily lost. I find my most fulfilling moments through providing loving services to others. In this place, I feel the presence of community. I fill with love and have more to give back. My life is now an ebb and flow of giving and receiving. Upon discovering true love in my life, I am able to write this book and begin sharing and serving. My experiences with bipolar disorder, depression and anxiety provide me a foundation for making a difference in the world through understanding others, which is truly my heart's desire.

Step Nine—
Accepting Responsibility

With my newly found awareness I accepted that I have a part in creating everything that happens and has happened in my life. The discovery of this gem of truth has allowed me to take total responsibility for all my experiences. I am no longer at the whim others! Whenever I experience problems, I now know that it is a reflection of what is in me. In the moment a problem arises, I have two choices. I can react and get sucked into the problems, or I can let go and observe. I find that the letting-go choice is much more beneficial for me. I experience less stress as a result and can process problems in hours rather than days or weeks. Every day I devote time and practice to clearing out old memories that can get in my way and show up as problems. I have collected some wonderful resources along the way (Ho'oponopono, a Hawaiian problem-solving process; neuro-linguistic programming; kundalini yoga) to support this practice and find them to be priceless!

Step Ten—
Falling in Love with Me

I mentioned early in Step Eight about trust in my relationship with myself. My experience with this is that it comes in waves. Little by little, my relationship with myself grows, just as with other relationships in my life. During Step Eight I focused on understanding that I needed to have a relationship with myself. During subsequent steps, I have been building that relationship. I have come to understand that there are three parts of me: subconscious (data center), conscious mind (intellect), and superconscious (higher self). When all three work in harmony, my life flows and works wonderfully. When any of the three parts are out of sync my life becomes a little awkward and hard.

My focus has shifted from needing to constantly be "doing" to learning how to "just be." By freeing myself from huge expectations to produce I have opened a space is in which love for myself grows. In this space love replaces self-loathing and nagging thoughts of how to fully become what I am expected to be. I love myself as I am. I am what I will become, at least for now. I will continue to grow and develop. In the meantime I enjoy my own company, something formerly out of reach for me. Me, myself and I are a one-person play! It is wonderful, joyous and life-fulfilling.

Because I have learned to balance my life I write from a fully grounded place. I have deep roots and yet I can reach high above my head into the sensations beyond sight, sound, touch, taste and smell. I can now access all of the beauty I experienced during manic episodes—without the accompanying outrageous behaviors that left a path of destruction.

Step Eleven—
Practicing Prayer and Meditation

I have never been religious. I consider myself spiritual but not religious. I do not find the need to be guided by a third party into relationship with God. Nurturing a god relationship is a personal journey, unique to every person. I am sure that there is an energetic presence to the universe, and sometimes I can feel it coursing through my body. I notice it during synchronistic encounters throughout my day. I hear it as an inspired thought in my mind. Sometimes I just feel that it is there—always there—shimmering in the silence, waiting to be called upon as a creative source in my life.

Every day I set aside time to be with myself and be silent. I never do it the same way twice. Among my many practices are journaling, pondering a quote or poem that resonates with me, listing to music, chanting mantras, watching the grass grow or the clouds float by, taking a walk in nature, or simply following my breath.

Step Twelve—
Waking Up

After everything I have experienced, for me waking up is the easy part. Staying awake is where fun begins! I still experience things that take me away from my center. I have moments of instability, as we all do. Learning to notice what takes me away and letting these things go takes constant vigilance on my part. My effort is well rewarded.

I have followed many paths of self help, and somewhere along the journey I finally learned that I'm not a project. I'm not broken or flawed. I am whole and perfect exactly as I am. Since I'm no longer a project, I am no longer working hard to get somewhere. For the first time I am happy to be exactly where I am: fully engaged and present in the here and now. Many well-meaning teachings relay that there is a long and rigid journey to follow to get a glimpse of heaven, nirvana or our Shangri-la. I have found my Shangri-la and it is within me, where it has always been. I have discovered that the only journey I need to take is the one that takes me deep within myself. I choose whether my experience is heavenly or hellish. It's up to me.

The Journey of a Thousand Miles Begins with a Single Step

Getting well happens gradually over a period of time. It's the small incremental steps that accumulate and one day you wake up and you feel lighter and less dense. The veil has lifted and you can breathe a little easier. During the process of getting well you will probably not always want to take the steps, you won't feel like it and you certainly will not see the point. However, with all that said, going through the motions will be beneficial in the long run.

Let me first address the conversation about whether you are worthy or deserve to have a successful life. If you are like me, you may be experiencing thinking that says you are not worthy. At one time you had great promise and potential but not now. You have been reduced to nothing more than a lump of uselessness and you are a complete waste of time and energy. This is all part of the depression weighing down on you. It's not who you are. Let me say that again. This is not who you are. You are not broken or bad or in any way lacking. You are in fact already whole and already perfect. Somehow you ended up where you are today. It's not important or relevant how you got here. It just happened, probably for myriad reasons, some of which you know and some that you don't. Forget the analysis and all the whys that it is or could be, and just begin to imagine that what I tell you may have some truth to it. You are perfect and whole and you can find your way back to a meaningful, purpose-filled, joyful life experience.

Consider for the moment the amazing capacity that you have as a human being. At any moment there are thousands of processes going on outside your conscious, yet you are alive and breathing, pumping, digesting and circulating. Your body is incredible; it has wisdom of its own. To get well you'll have to take the journey into your body-, mind- and spirit-wisdom all at once. You can't get there with your head alone; all parts of you must integrate and work in conjunction with each other.

The fact that you are now suffering from depression, anxiety or bipolar disorder is an effect of past neglect of yourself. Your neglect of yourself got so bad that your mind had to shut down in order to get your attention. Please don't let this burden you more. In all honesty we live in a culture that calls us selfish if we get too interested in our own needs. It's no surprise that you, like millions of others, didn't see the signs and are now stuck in the murky depths of despair. I am so sorry this has happened to you. Please forgive yourself and love yourself and perhaps one day you can even thank yourself.

If this is not the first time you've gotten stuck, don't despair. Remember in my story there are three major depressions in a five-year period. It took me a while to see the whole picture. What is going on with you is NOT a life sentence. There is hope. At this moment, or any you choose, you can begin to think and create a different tomorrow.

Join the Conversation

This is not the end of the story but rather the beginning of your story. We all begin again from this moment. You may be drawn to learn more about how to rid your own life of depression or someone close to you. Perhaps you are called to help with the larger conversation of how to rid the world of depression. Whatever your calling, log onto www.thedepressionproject.com to join our community and continue the journey.

Afterward: Reflecting on Mental Illness

Because of past incidents in my life, I have created boundaries that are difficult to cross. I continue to have a hard time letting people in, even to this day. My situation, however, is not unique. The capacity to feel pain and suffering, as well as joy and laughter, is a common trait across humanity. Everyone creates a life of his or her own, with conditions, walls, doors, and windows. The "house" through which people; and situations come and go frames our experiences and shapes our lives. Reading my story, you pass through my house, and experience the perspective from which I look, and have looked, out upon the world.

It has been almost ten years since my last episode of mania or depression. It has been seven years since I've taken a drop of medication for bipolar disorder. I know now that there is no way I walked my path alone. I had help, lots of help. When I could not keep myself out of harm's way, something reached in and saved me. In the beginning, before clinical depression had really taken hold of me, I wrote about the fact that I would be writing this very book. I did not have a clue that I was heading into the experience I had, but I knew I was going to write a book. I am sure God's hand has been in my life.

I would never have directed my life into mental illness, but I would not trade the insight I have learned from taking the journey. The process of writing this book has been incredibly healing for me. It is only now, ten years on, that I'm able to revisit some of the dark places in which I lived for five years. As I dropped in to tell a piece of the story, I was able to feel the depth of my experience once again, only this time I could face it without running. I still felt afraid at times. Some of the emotional states in which I have been are painful and not fun to revisit. Telling my story has given me the opportunity to face all of my fears and reclaim any final lost fragments of my being. My wounds are healed and I am whole again.

Medication Does Not Bring Healing

As I reflect back on this period of my life I believe that my story, although extreme, is also the story of so many other people. If you really look around the world, it seems to be a place of complete insanity. It is unsurprising that people are fragmented and disoriented. The world is fragmented and disoriented. If you have any feelings at all, the idea of such extreme suffering of so many can be too much to bear. Disconnecting from your feelings and from the world all together seems like a good idea.

Mental illness has reached epidemic levels. The standard answer to the problem is to medicate. Millions worldwide are now medicated beyond reason. Medication is about functionality, not healing. Medication merely serves to numb the symptoms and suppress the root cause of the pain. However, it is impossible to hide forever from hurts and pains of unhealed wounds. We have all had experiences that have left their mark. For some the marks are visible as scars on the outside. For others the scars are all on the inside, sheltered from view.

Guilt and suffering are two feelings that unite the entire human race. All cultures program guilt and obedience to a societal norm as a means of keeping control. The result is that everyone has a need to move beyond feelings of unworthiness, self-loathing and guilt. It is time for all of us to stop searching outside of ourselves for answers. It is time to stop listening to what others think is the right path for each individual. It is time for us to turn and take the journey inward. In the silence of our hearts we learn about love and the flow of life. We are our own saviors. We can't save others. We only need to save ourselves. Melissa Etheridge sings "I need to Wake Up." This is my wish for you. Take courage and hope. Wake up. Life is waiting. Wake up. You are needed. Wake up. Give your love to the world. Its all there is to do.

Healing Requires Collecting the Fragments of Ourselves

One might describe the fragmented mind during mental illness as a conflict between the face we show to the world and the face we keep hidden. During mental illness the need to hide is intensified as our hidden, shadow side has somehow leaked through, unleashing the ugliness of our psyche for the whole world to see. When others see our shadow side it might scare them because they recognize our experience in themselves. People will ostracize the mentally ill because those people show others a side they are unwilling to recognize in themselves.

Reclaiming the pieces of your self and putting them back together takes courage and effort. What you seek is a place of unity within your self so that you can accept all of you as you are. You have to believe, for your self, that every part of you is perfect the way it is. You must believe that you are unique and your perspective is needed in the world; that without you a vital part of consciousness would be missing. This is not an overnight accomplishment, but more of a daily practice of working toward wholeness.

I intend my story to be a message of hope—to relay the message that it is possible to find a way through suffering and darkness and out of fear. You can find peace in your life. You can meet yourself in the middle—that center place between the highs and the lows. The place is known by many names: balance, center, the zone. You will move in and out of the middle, but after you find it once the power to find your way back is always within you.

The Gift of the Self

There are no more maps, no more creeds, no more philosophies. From here on in, the direction comes straight from the Divine. The curriculum is being revealed millisecond by millisecond—invisibly, intuitively, spontaneously, lovingly. As one of Thomas Merton's monks has it, "Go into your cell and your cell will teach you everything there is to know." Your cell. Your self.

—Akshara Noor

The Depression Project
Rid the World of Depression...
Join the Conversation

www.thedepressionproject.com

"For every complex problem there is a simple solution. And it's wrong."

–Anonymous

With depression reaching pandemic levels, the suffering of so many people is devastating. People are losing large segments of their life to the dis-ease of melancholy and its companions, mania and anxiety. The causes of depression are complex and vary from one individual to another. Our continued search for the quick fix or "silver bullet" is not working. More and more people are being diagnosed and treated for depression, bipolar and anxiety everyday. With these increasing numbers, it's time for a radically new approach to these seemingly unsolvable problems of society.

The Depression Project is focused on helping people attain balance and peace of mind. It assumes that these very states are our birthright and we can find our way to them through relationship with ourselves, community with others and an understanding of how our remarkable human body works.

The Depression Project aims to provide people access to resources that impact the states of depression, mania and anxiety. Offering inspiration, hope and "how to" information to anyone wanting to recover from these mental illnesses rather than pander to symptom management.

The resources offered here do not come with side effects; only the possibility of complete restoration of balance and peace of mind. Join the conversation and be part of ridding the world of depression.

Help people recover so that the world may receive the benefi t of their gifts and talents. Every single person's contribution is important and their ability to share should never be masked by these mental illnesses or marginalized by the current forms of traditional treatment.

Useful Resources

This list includes books that I found personally very beneficial on my own journey. It is intended to provide a starting point for people on their own road to wellness for more resources please go to www.thedepressionproject.com

A Guide to Spiritual Enlightenment by Eckhart Tolle; ©1999 Eckhart Tolle; New World Library, Novato, CA/Namaste Publishing, Vancouver; ISBN 1-57731-480-8

Angels Within Us: A spiritual guide to the twenty-two angels that govern our lives by John Randolph Price; ©1993 John Randolph Price; A Fawcett Columbine Book published by Ballantine Books, New York; ISBN 0-449-90784-8

Ask and It Is Given: Learning to Manifest Your Desires by Esther and Jerry Hicks; ©2004; Hay House, Inc., Carlsbad, CA; ISBN 1-4019-0459-9

Awakening the Buddha Within: Tibetan Wisdom for the Western World by Lama Surya Das; ©1997 Lama Surya Das; Broadway Books, division of Bantam Doubleday Dell Publishing Group, NY; ISBN 0-7679-0157-6

HeartMath Solution: The Institute of HeartMath's Revolutionary Program for Engaging the Power of the Heart's Intelligence by Doc Lew Childre and Howard Martin; ©1999 The Istitute of HeartMath; Harper Collins Publishers, Inc., NY; ISBN 0-06-251606-X

Love without Conditions: Reflections of the Christ Mind by Paul Ferrini; Heartways Press, Greenfield, MA; ISBN 1-879159-15-5

Radical Forgiveness: Making Room for the Miracle by Colin C. Tipping; ©2002 Colin C. Tipping; Global 13 Publications, Inc., Marietta, GA; ISBN 0-9704814-1-1

The Laws of Spirit: A Tale of Transformation by Dan Millman; ©1995 Dan Millman; An H.J. Kramer Book published in a joint venture with New World Library, Novato, CA; ISBN 0-915-811-93-6

The Power of Intention by Wayne W. Dyer; ©2004 Wayne W. Dyer; Hay House, Inc., Carlsbad, CA; ISBN 1-4019-0216-2

You Can Heal Your Life by Louise L. Hay; ©1984, 1987, 2004 Louise L. Hay; Hay House, Inc., Carlsbad, CA; ISBN 0-937611-01-8

Zero Limits: The Secret Hawaiian System for Wealth, Health, Peace, and More by Joe Vitale and Ihaleakala Hew Len; ©2007; John Wiley & Sons, Inc., Hoboken, NJ; ISBN 978-0-470-10147-6

Journals and other Writings...

The Beginning of Madness

This is the beginning of my Journal, the purpose of which is to make a permanent record of my thoughts and feelings in an effort to understand myself better and achieve greater clarification in my communications with others.

Today is Tuesday 3rd October 1995. I am presently travelling north bound to Newcastle where a world of fear and excitement awaits me.

I am feeling slightly empty and alone for what was my home is no longer, what was my life is changing, what lies ahead off me is unknown. Mixed with the sadness is anticipation and excitement. I have the power and freedom to create whatever life I want. My only constraint for the next three years is it must be in Newcastle.

This I believe is a good thing as it does not allow me to do what I always do and run away or run off with another man!

Well it's been a while. It is now 30th March 1996 and I'm 24 now. Things have moved on rapidly in the last few months. The stakes feel high and I've got the perspective keeping me away from everyone - only this time. Mr Wonderful is there too. It is true that we are really alone in this world and we must create all for ourselves. I want to go home and I know I must press forward beyond this shit place to a more beautiful, enlightened place beyond the uncertainty. Transition is a tough call.

Where to from here?

Tuesday 23rd April 1996 - I'm working through everything. Right Now I am in total survival mode - to the point of anger + frustration about the business - Clive's business, the flat - all the bits that aren't perfect yet. It seems the only way I can get people to listen is by getting mad. Tomorrow is the day I will sort out the approach to the bank - good news/bad news and where to next! It's time to get in control of the financial position both business + personal. I remember doing this in Jan & the viability was difficult to find. It will be a very different picture +

to be honest - I am finding it hard to create good work without a clear direction.

Financially, I am on the jagged edge of bankruptcy. And must look after my own position first & foremost.

I'm tired of creating for the creditors & not having a bean to keep my own house in order.

I'm searching for an objective place w/out responsibility for everyone else. I'm sure w/ a rest & a good night's sleep it will be there in the morning, turning negative energy into positive solutions.

My life is in shambles.
Lots of people have offered
their help and support
and all I do is reject
everyone's HELP. WHAT?

Anna what on earth are you
doing, what is it that you want
and how are you going to
get the help you need?

You really are not dealing
with your life at all well.
There are several things that
you require

Why are you denying yourself
all the pleasures of life -
you could be living life to the full

The problems are great the opportunities are becoming more and more limited.

How did I lose sight of living life to the full - what can I do to get it back again?

Why am I refusing to get well - what on earth am I going to do with myself.

It's horrible, I do not have any kind of quality of life and I am not sure how to get it back.

I need to see a counsellor pretty quickly - maybe they can shed some light

Something inside of me is suggesting that I document my experiences of the last few months (May-Sept 1996). What a very strange experience it has been and not something I wish to go through again in my life.

25:10:96

I have spent the last view months reflecting upon my experiences and have come up with several snap shot phrases that really sum it up for me. Though being our experience those doon will not evoke the same understanding in others, so I think I'll have to dig a little deeper!

It's a strange thing but I'm not sure how to label the experience. It wasn't really a nervous breakdown but certainly a breakdown of the mind.

The doctors labelled it 'Clinic Depression'.

My mind became completely fragmented. Nothing made sense anymore, nothing was easy and nothing had any meaning or point to it.

It was only when I started to recover that I think I began to realise how ill I had been.

I would say now as I am writing this I have (eclined) to laugh + cry again am functioning normally yet not fully recovered.

I am still looking back at the experience and am slightly fearful of being thrown back there.

Journals and other Writings...

The Kelowna Letters

~~genuine improvements that~~
~~can create a difference to the~~
~~bottom line~~

~~The search for quality - why~~
~~settle for anything else~~

~~Feeling better !~~

How is it possible to move forward. from here? I have gone so far into my head that I can not see any kind of future with me in it... My mom is trying to help me. Everyone has been trying to help me - I'm supposed to help myself. To get **well.**

It is easier to consider not getting well. I want to

go home – I can at least try
to make a difference there but
I have no money to go anywhere
or do anything. This is happens
because I made it happen,
but why? I do not want
to live on into the future
alone, without anything of
my own – I do not see how
I can do any of this from here.
I have hurt too many
people.

Please, let me dye (die) and then. I can rest in peace. How else can I make ammends. with my friends + family. My mom is a good person — She doesn't deserve me. The walls are too high in all directions. I loved everyone in my life that I said I loved - that was never a lie. and now I must set everyone free. - let them mourn + grieve & then heal. for the loss of of me — There is no forward for me.

— Anna Maiden, was once +
now is no more.

What could the future look
like? Work, work, work,
work, work, work, work.
+ no play, no fun, no joy.

What happened to me?

I want to be back where I was
a few months ago and do
it all a little differently.

IT'S TIME TO GO — TO LEAVE
THIS WORLD AND BE IN ANOTHER
DIMENSION.

6

Mom,

I am feeling much better today, except for the fact that I can not share your life with you, not this way.

This is causing far too much stress for you and is not the place I need to be to get really + fully well.

I would ask of you one final favour and I will find a way to repay you. Please lend me the money to get back home. - (I will sell what I can to repay you Daddy).

I need to go and face my fears, salvage whatever I can of who I have been and what has been created, so that I can rebuild a future again for all of us. You, Darren, Yvette and of course me.

This is not the way - I know you are worried about me but I've always been okay and I will continue to be okay

If I stay here I will not get better - there is too much of a world of pain & suffering surrounding everyone here

If I do not go home my fears will continue to eat my alive and you too.

mom

You asked where will I go when I get home - the answer is, to any number of the friends I have there, just as you have here.

It is time for me to go back to work, doing the work I love to do - helping other people create possibilities in their lives for happiness.

I will create happiness for myself and thus in turn for the people who love and care for me.

For you, you need to let me go and do what I have to do.

There are people waiting for you to find happiness and your own too.

I would ask you to come with me but I know that's not practical or realistic.

Anna is asking this of you so as she can face herself. If I do not do this now, I will not be able to live with me - for there is no peace in running away.

This, I hope makes some sense. And I am sorry to have caused you heartache. We have got to be good friends over the years and there will be many more happy moments for us. I just must do what I must do.

enough of being sick and unwell - I am better, well enough to go and do what I should of done some months ago.

I will eat and rest appropriately and keep in regular contact with you to let you know I am okay. And I will love Anna again.

This is not my attempt at trying to save the world this is the only chance I have to save myself and my family.

I am prepared to be starting again close to you and Darren + Yvette, but must go home and close the loops I have opened first of all.

Please do not be upset (I know you will!) but this is the only way I can have any sanity of mind for myself and this in turn for other people.

I understand that there is no business however, there is still available the information on my accomplishments and many people who can put me back to work in the field I love. 'facilitating personal growth.'

The grieving period is over and the doing period is here. It is not productive to be angry at the others - everyone is doing their best including you + I.

4

I'm not trying to fix something that
can not be fixed I know much of it
is beyond repair but I am not
if I can only go and face the
days with those who are involved
(i.e.
+ a whole host of other people).

We are meant to experience much
joy and happiness together beyond
this place. I am not like you,
only a part of you.

This is not meant to push you
to the edge, honestly I want us
to be happy together as a family
but it must be a better way
than this.

One better way is to have ~~every~~
Anna back on track again full of
the joy of living and striving to
good work in the world for those
closest and those who are less
fortunate.

My mind is coming back together
quicker that expected!

I love you
dearly.

Anna

Journals and other Writings...

1997 Post Hospital...

Here we are again more than 12 months on and back to square one. I keep thinking that it is all so hard - does it really have to be this hard. I feel like I've missed out on a 2nd summer to mental illness. How do I find my way back - and quickly. I feel so much pain and isolation in this nightmare I just want the pain to stop and life to be filled with joy and happiness. Why did I have to slip over the edge - it doesn't seem fair - twice now I've been brought to my knees and must struggle to stand up again - where do I find my own piece of happiness - difficult to say when you don't know where to look. I'm always seeking the next step

Is it the right move, will things get better away from here or will it be just a different kind of hell.

Why do I cry so much, I hold so much pain for all that is past & much that is present

Please reach

Oh. Anna,
What have you done to yourself. You get further and further away from everyone and everything each day. No one can do it for you & can really help you - you must help yourself. The question is but "How?" as each day passes it is a little piece of time which can not be retrieved ever - is it all unimportant or is this a hell you are keeping yourself in. Where to from here. It is all so black and dim it does not seem fair - have I made so many wrong moves

Anna,

It seems everyone is pushing you to put your life back together. There is so much to do, a new home, a job you want to do, friends, extra curricular activities - what exactly are you waiting for?

There is nothing to wait for. Face the facts, you've lost just about everything - it is time to start over.

On the grounds that you have little or no idea about what you want to do, just get busy.

If there is no meaning in your life then go and find some meaning.

I think patience has all but run dry now = you must get up & get on.

Search for the Hero Inside Yourself.
Only you have the answers to unlock your own life & find happiness.

I am so alone now - everyone has left me to go to sleep or do whatever I feel like. I guess they just don't understand or know what to do.

The drugs are making me less able to cope not more able.

Should I stay here in London which I absolutely hate and despise where I know only my family & their friends. It is not the easiest of cities to have new beginnings in.

As for ▮▮▮▮ and I, I just don't know. He seems to have more time to help out Tom than me. He is the only one I can talk to. but I spend half my time being angry that he hasn't sorted things out properly.

What happens - we move into a
flat we need someone elses guarantee.
Can we get a telephone etc. Can
we live a somewhat normal life?
I have my doubts about this.

I am not even in a position
to purchase new knickers -
never mind clothes which are
coming to their end as
well. I put my faith in
some one to look after me
when I could not (can not)
look after myself and it
does not seem to be achieve-
able.

What can I do - work is too
big of a step right now so it
seems I have no choice. Whilst
in this position things get worse
and worse for me everyday.

The only option is to get well enough
to go to work and then do it for

myself - which is what I've always done - except when ill

Some partnership - I only see money if I ask for it - how degrading.

Again, we're in a position of having to pay wages before we see any money and we don't have a dime! What is going on.

I cannot drive as a result of the drugs I'm taking - nor do I have anywhere to drive to.

Things are not picking up in the way I had hoped by coming to London - I don't know - maybe Texas is the better option. Good food, good weather and friendly people.
  - Personal Survival -

They don't even speak to me here.

What is happening - am I truely invisible

I think so.

Journals and other Writings...

Letter from Mom...

My Dearest Anna,

I will endeavor to put into writing the love I have for you so you will have something to carry in you pocket as a gentle reminder. I wish with all my heart that the pain of aloneness will leave your mind and that the smile will return to your face. I believe that surrounded by love you can make that happen.

I would hope to see you go into therapy in New York to assist you over these difficult times - Please let someone help you Anna - I am not the one as you are far too angry with me at the present. I will assist from the background - be assured that I am always there and that I will be praying for you every hour. Please put your trust in the Lord and place your problems at his feet and he will guide you out of the darkness of loneliness - just remember you are never really alone - the Lord is always with you.

You mentioned to me that your soul is dying - that is not possible as your soul was created by God and he takes care of all souls - your mind is not listening to him at the moment, but he is still there watching over you. Open your heart to God Anna and he will help you to make your life beautiful. You are a beautiful and talented young woman and you have so much to offer in this world.

In your letter you said that all you have done is cause me heartache and grief an disappointment - that is not so Anna, I have many joyful memories of us together, from the moment of your conception to the recent past - Now I feel a great sadness and anger at having lost our joy to whatever demons haunt your mind at the present. I will not pretend that I am not upset about some of the problems that keep coming back to haunt us - but I am pretty tough and I will survive. We will survive together if you will trust that we all love you and want you to be with us. Just reach out your hand and we'll be there with support and hugs.

I love you Anna I cannot do better than that - love is the strongest power I know and you are surrounded by love from your family - bask in the warmth of that love and your strength will return.

I have three magic wishes left and I give them to you - I wish you health, wealth and the happiness of love forever and ever.

All My Love
Mom

Journals and other Writings...

London 1998 – Letter to Mom

My Life

The future's so bright I've got to wear shades, this I know,
For confusion brings clarity, thus forward I go.

As the chaos of present time fades,
I truly know I've got to wear shades.

Until I see the sun shine bright,
I'll rest in the knowledge that all will come right.

For the day will dawn when the grey clouds lift,
And I will see life as the ultimate gift.

Dearest mom,

Its time for me to put pen to paper again!

I'm sorry that my father contacted you in the way he did. It must be very difficult to keep that chapter closed for you as he doesn't seem to give up easily.

Something positive came from it though. And I believe it started a process of communication between you & I which is long overdue.

I'm sorry I didn't come to you and ask for what I needed. I do feel well overdrawn with you not just financially but more importantly emotionally.

I feel very guilty about the way I have treated you over the last three years,

You have always been there for me and on many occasions I've thrown your kindness back in your face.

I made a promise to myself & I now make it to you also that no one will ever be able to drive a wedge between us again.

I want you to know that I am making a commitment to try & put right many of the wrongs I have done for example: I will be approaching Don about the money I owe him & find a way to repay that debt.

I'm working hard not to put too much pressure on myself; I feel that if I don't right the wrongs I've done I'll continue to carry bad karma & won't be able to sleep straight in my bed at night.

I often say "it's hard being me". This it true & its not a self pity statement. I have the ability to swim in all different kinds of life's streams some good & some bad. Swimming upstream in the main stream is a real challenge for me & I'm committed to get it right this time.

I keep reminding myself that fundementally I am a good person who has chosen to walk some dodgy paths which have landed me in deep water without a life jacket, boat or padel!

I can honestly say that I don't look back with too many regrets as I believe its all part of the process of finding myself & ultimately fulfilling my goals. In case you don't remember what they are I'll remind you!

I want to help people make a difference in their lives through coaching, lecturing, training & counselling. When I leave this world I want to go in the knowledge that I've made a positive difference.

To achieve this goal with integrity & congruence I need to truely learn to walk the walk, not just talk the talk! I do however give myself permission not to be perfect, after all I'm only human.

Anyway enough about me, lets talk about you & us.

I remember a time when we were best g friends, providing encouragement & support to each other. I miss this, + want to work towards re-bonding with you + putting some balance back in our relationship.

I think the key to achieving this is to open up the communication lines between us fully. let's be honest & say how we feel - No more walking on eggshells.

I am really looking forward to moving to Texas + being close to you again. I think we do have fun sometimes, right?

Maybe we can find a way together to earn a living & have

fun doing it.

My optimism & your realism
combined might be a great
combination!

You never can tell what the
future holds.

I do know this - you better
buy yourself a set of extra
strong shades. The future's
bright & we're all gonna
be okay.

I love you dearly & I'll
See you soon.

Your daughter

Anna

PS I'm here, I'm ready & I'm getting
stronger everyday.

Journals and other Writings...

San Francisco Postcards

PAINTINGS by

FEBRUARY 7TH - MARCH 14TH SHOWING AT
Quetzal – 1234 Polk Street at Bush - SECA 94109
415-673-4181 to go ext 14   415-673-4182 Fax
E-Mail- quetzal@quetzal.org   Web- http://www.quetzal.org/

Get the world's Finest Coffee and Cocoa ONLINE

I Never lied
about being
all of you.

Fill this
VOID
Postally

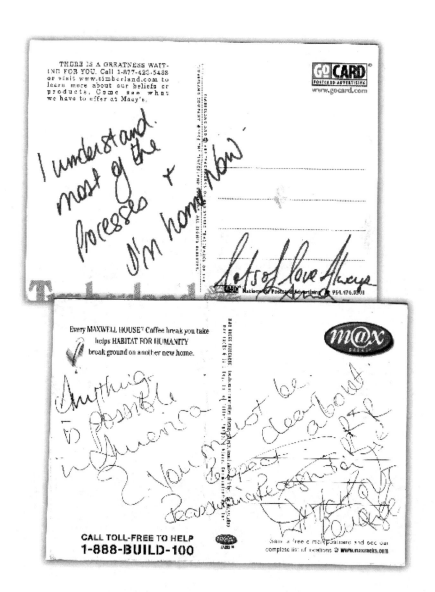

I understand most of the Processes +
I'm home Now.

lots of love Always

Anything is possible in America

You must be dear about

respect

Passionate

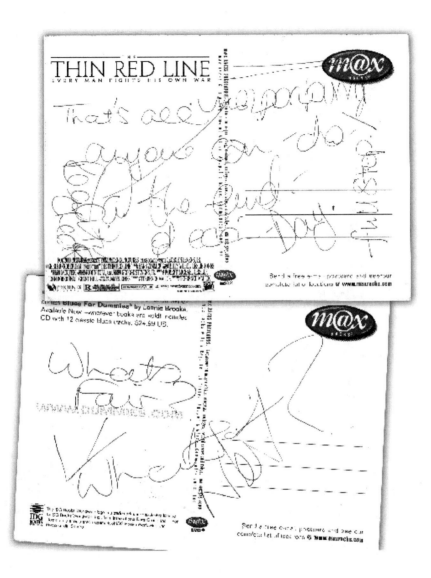

Journals and other Writings...

San Francisco Hospital

INVOLUNTARY PATIENT ADVISEMENT
(TO BE READ AND GIVEN TO THE PATIENT AT TIME OF ADMISSION)

MH 300 E/S (3/87)

Name of Facility _SFGH_

Patient's Name _ANNA MAIDEN_   Admission Date _2-3-99_

Section 5157 (c) and (d) of the Welfare and Institutions Code (W&I) requires that each person admitted for 72-hour evaluation be given specific information orally and in writing, and a record of the advisement be kept in the patient's medical record.

My name is _DONNA_

My position here is _NURSE_

You are being placed in this psychiatric facility because it is the opinion of the professional staff, that as a result of a mental disorder, you are: (check applicable)

Dangerous to yourself ___✓___

Dangerous to others _____

Gravely Disabled (unable to
provide for your own food,
clothing or shelter) ___✓___

Document specific evidence which substantiates reason for hold:

We feel this is true because _You were yelling + screaming in a restaurant, had no sleep + missed flight home to Texas._

You will be held for a period of up to 72 hours. This (does not) (does) include weekends or holidays. Your 72-hour period will begin: _2-3-99 at 0925_ (Time and Date). Your 72-hour evaluation and treatment period will end at: _2-5-99 at 0925_ (Time and Date).

During these 72 hours you will be evaluated by the hospital staff, and the treatment you receive may include medications. It is possible for you to be released before the end of the 72 hours, but if the professional staff decide that you need continued treatment, you can be held for a longer period of time. If you are held longer than 72 hours, you have the right to a lawyer and a qualified interpreter and a hearing before a judge. If you are unable to pay for the lawyer, then one will be provided free.

State law presumes you to be competent regardless of whether you have been evaluated or treated for mental disorder as a voluntary or involuntary patient.

Good Cause for Incomplete Advisement	Date

Advisement Completed By	Position	Date
Donna	Nurse	2-3-99

CC: Original to the Patient
Carbon to Patient's Record

NOTICE OF CERTIFICATION

The authorized agency providing evaluation services in the County of San Francisco has evaluated the condition of:

Name _____ Anna HALDEN _____

Address _____ San Antonio, Tx _____

Age __26__ Sex __F__ Marital Status __Single__

We, the undersigned, allege that the above-named person is, as a result of mental disorder or impairment by chronic alcoholism:

    (1) a danger to others.

    (2) a danger to himself or herself.

    (3) gravely disabled as defined in paragraph (1) of subdivision (h) or subdivision (1) of Section 5008 of the Welfare and Institutions Code. [Strike out all inapplicable classifications.]

The specific facts which form the basis for our opinion that the above-named person meets one or more of the classifications indicated above are as follow: (certifying persons to fill in blanks)

Disorganized, cannot formulate convincing plan for provision of shelter or food or clothing.

The above-named person has been informed of this evaluation, and has been advised of the need for, but has not been able or willing to accept treatment on a voluntary basis, or to accept referral to, the following services:

SFGH Inpatient Service, Unit 7B

We, therefore, certify the above-named person to receive intensive treatment related to the mental disorder or impairment by chronic alcoholism for no more than 14 days, beginning this __5th__ day of __Feb__ 19 99 in the intensive treatment facility herein named:

Unit 7B, SFGH

We hereby state that a copy of this notice has been delivered this day to the above-named person, and that he/she has been informed of his/her legal right to a judicial review by Habeas Corpus, and this term has been explained to him/her, and that he/she has been informed of his/her right to counsel, including court appointed counsel pursuant to Section 5276 of the Welfare and Institutions Code.

We hereby state that a copy of this notice has been delivered by _____
and that the patient, when advised of his/her rights to a judicial review, (requested such review) (did not request such review). [Cross out one]

Date _____ 2/5/99 _____

Signature _____

Countersignature _____

I hereby state that I delivered a copy of this notice this day to the above-named person and that I informed him/her that a certification review hearing will be held within four days and that an attorney or advocate will visit him/her to provide assistance in preparing for the hearing or to answer questions regarding his or her commitment or to provide other assistance.

Signed _____ Date _____ 2/5/99 _____

MHS 1536SF

Individual Ca   Plan

My doctor on 7B is ▮▮▮▮▮

— My Social Worker is ▮▮▮▮▮ —Taking Rob's place

— The Occupational Therapist is ▮▮▮▮▮

— My Nurses are _Chuck, ____ O▮ET - Student Pharm._

___ Medical Student: ▮▮▮▮▮

My Diagnosis is _Bi-Polar Affective Disorder_
                      (Defective)

I often have these symptoms _____
misplaced anger, hyper activity (difficulty sleeping)
I get agitated + need to change something
(anything) - Seem important to keep busier ever
if late for all matters ✱ Severe depression fear of confined
spaces, hyper sensitive to ▮▮▮▮
Some things I can do to make the symptoms
better are _Distraction, Reading, Sleeping,_
Walking, working, Smoking, drinking,
Singing, laughing, dancing

I usually come into the hospital because _____
Someone demands it of me, it is
another forced issue based on
my belief of other's expectations

My doctor has prescribed these medications
DEPAKOTE (MANIA). ANTI-tic . MOTRIN (IBU) .
ZYPREXA (MANIA) ANYCOTIC . ATIVAN (LESS ANXIOUS).
PREVENT

I have these side effects from the medications
DOUBLE VISION | SHAKES. | Sore tongue (Rare.
On both sides.)

mouth
Thrush

I can manage these side effects by
Rest, Work + Play - occupying time
in different ways.

When I leave the hospital I will have these supports

mother
Nurse < Name Ann Marie Malden (RN)

med
student < Name_____ (Texas/friend)

Financial aid < Name_____
friend

I will have psychiatric follow-up with
_____
Address___Unknown.
     Phone_____ Decision will be
                         made with immediate
                         family members.

page 160

MY GOALS IN THE HOSPITAL

I will reach these two goals before I leave 7B:

1) I will control my anxiety attacks.
with methods I am clear about + now use.

2. I will get the necessary answers.
I require when I need them.

My SHORT TERM GOAL for this week is: (You can set this in O.T. Goal Setting Group)

1) To Eat, Sleep, Drink, (Smoke Cigs),
Breath the fresh air go home before
1 miss another family event.

My DAILY GOALS are:

DAY AND DATE	GOALS	OUTCOMES

Early warning signs for me are

Brick, anxiety, anger, frustration, boredom.
Shakes, aggressive behaviour

When I have any of these early warning signs I will

Stop doing what I'm doing & find
~~another way~~ *way to relax. deal wl*
my own issues privately

After I leave the hospital I can relax by_____ .

meditation, walking, sining, reading,
sleeping etc
_____ → *Variety of activities*
Staying away or resting

After I leave the hospital I can have fun by_____

As above — Laughing alot

If I need help with money I will call
ANN MARIE MALDEN

APPENDIX H:

Journals and other Writings...

San Antonio, Texas

FRIDAY 26TH FEBRUARY. - VICKI Adam.

† If you keep doing what you're doing,
you will get what you've got!

† Actions Speak louder than words.

† Positive / feedback

Health does not come
from a state of
preperativing Ulang

List Associatios

* Coffee pot needs cleaning

uncomplete
thought
process.

No leave it ←
* I might break it

Suggested
Reading
HOWARD
MARKS
Me Rice

lack some
sense of personal
responsibility

option

break replace

Blocked thoughts

Clutter
can't think
concentrate
focus.

* Back track

follow through
is only way
out.

walk in
a room
can't remember
what for

* unstick the thoughts

Solid Foundation

Rejection is all they do not need

To Avoid

Recognition
Respect
Reassurance

Growth ≠ VS Comfort Zone

Make changes gradually
makings
Changes = taking risks

Handle It
Evaluate consequences

What do I have Right Now? (likes/dislikes)

(Change) - Personal Hatred

to Bld a person you like, love
then the other steps
will follow.

Potential to overcome
malfunction

Brain Transplants: whatever
the malfunction, correct it

- Chemistry
- Biological
- Social

Behaviour changes

Behaviour
modification

✗ Lithium is a
natural salt

Anti Convulsives,
Depakote

Symptom Controllers

1st line of change is medication

2nd "   "   "   Coping mechanisms

3rd "   "   "   Communication

→ Stress Mgnt

Triangles

with self
with others
in groups

Dynamics

competitiveness.

Moderation
is healthy

win/win or on
deal (negotiation)

Grieving process

James - SW

Interpersonal Relationships

1) It can be a major source of stress for most people.

Insecurity → maintain + control.
↓
Seek reassurance + validation from others.

Male/female Relationship of non-relatives tend to be most stressful.

FAMILY
BASE
"ANCHOR" → Anchored

Separation

Family Interactional Patterns that is disfunctional.
Positive people in environment.

endurance.

learn + attempt to solve own problems

Biological	Environmental	Psychosocial
Out of control	Subjective to possible change	Stressors
	supportive	

(Dt) Marginal in job/relationship/
(functional) responsibility

problem solving skills will decrease ↓

you are happy while you're happy

*gateway to hardcore & crime

w/ mental illness gas on slow
burning fire

3/3/99

Insight:-

* acute awareness of disease process

* thought processes → jumbled up

* motivation & determination to get well

- frustration of living with a
  disability people cannot see.

- trapped in own head
  with negative or positive
  thoughts.

- multiple stimuli → compounded
  into greater →

I would

exacerbation/ — decompensation
  opposites   of previous
remission   condition

out of control / under control

Thursday 4/3/99.

{ Still Can't take a bus ride
{ All By Myself

Quite an adventurous morning,
I achieved my primary goal
early on, to get a Carelink card,
which now entitles me to
community health care based
on my ability to pay. Hooray!

I walked from the Hospital
to the River Centre Mall taking
in the sites, sounds + attractions
along the way > Getting lost + unlost several times!

San Antonio early morning
is different. I spotted the
homeless, spoke with the
Ranger had the worst
M'Donalds ever + watched how
the people here put Tourism together.

Mixing the familiar with
the unfamiliar made it
exciting + I stayed away
from the crowds.

Just Noticing People, the
environment + keeping a check
on the Time!

3-13-99

It has been an extremely
successful week

Monday: Computer training
            @ Community Centre
Tues-Fri: Full Time @ Girling
            doing Admin (Paid work)

Tomorrow will be exactly
one month since my release
from hospital

I stopped the Zyprexa from
monday & am managing
well without it.

I seem to be able to cope
in high stress well I feel
set back by the hospitalisation
for a number of reasons.

I wake up early morning feeling
ashamed of the behaviour I
displayed to God knows who in
San Franc.

14/3/99

Poot Wire's very plucky Birthday party.

Have have thoughts racing through my mind about the San Fran experience.

Some are clear others are still a little vague. I guess I need to ask some questions of Gary & the others I met to find out how bizarre it all really was.

The restaurant we went to eat at — what was it called — when I couldn't sit, stay & eat anything — I think they threw me out!

Sometimes you can put everything in place & it still goes to Shit!

Oh & Well Reality Bites!

3/15/99

Reality Bites Hard! Much activity +
busyness - it's been a long day @
work, the truth is I feel bug down

The Focus point needs to be, what
is right for "Anna"

Anna was clear when she left the
2k what the direction was, little
has alter, there have been some
laughs along the way & some
sorrow too.

Time is a natural healer

I'm free to do whatever I
want

20th March '99 - 1st day of Spring

Today is a very bad day - its beautiful weather & I'm sitting in the sunshine, yet the tears are running down my face.

I feel empty & alone & without the sense of purpose or how to fulfill any purpose which is what make other people responsive towards me.

"everblack" - then you really might know what its like

- Actions spk louder than words

About the Authors:

Anna Miller is an accomplished business consultant with fifteen years' experience consulting, coaching, and training her clients to achieve greater success for themselves and each other. She has a passion for making a difference in the world by igniting passion and bringing forth creativity of the people she works with. She loves to help her clients realize their potential and act in ways that change their world significantly . . .

Through sharing her story of recovery from bipolar disorder, depression and anxiety, she wants to help sufferers the world over find hope, inspiration and "how to" information that can help heal their life. The Depression Project, which she founded, provides access to resources and an ongoing dialogue about how to rid the world of depression.

Ann Marie Malden is a registered nurse and Dr, of Naturopathy. She is also a published poet, and most importantly Anna's mother. She was born in Canada, has lived, and traveled extensively, and currently resides in San Antonio, Texas. Ann Marie is a passionate supporter of the Depression Project, and lends her expertise from both an allopathic, and a naturopathic perspective. Together with her daughter she hopes to support depression sufferers and their families as they journey through the mental illness maze to wellness.